Facts from The Sleepwatchers: Lack of sleep is a bigger factor in accidents than alcohol. Your brain is more active when you're dreaming than when you're awake—it has to be. A big meal, a warm room, or a boring lecture won't put you to sleep—if you're getting enough to begin with.

There's a lot more to sleep than simply "turn in, tune out, and drop off," and Dr. William C. Dement, the dean of sleepwatchers, is just the one to talk about it. He is director of the Stanford University School of Medicine's Sleep Disorders Clinic—the world's first such facility—as well as the former chairman of the National Commission on Sleep Disorders Research, a position to which he was appointed by the U.S. Secretary of Health and Human Services.

This irreverent account retraces the history of modern sleep research from its infancy (featuring Dement as a young intern, hunched over sleeping hospital patients like "the Angel of Death dressed in white," trying to see if their eyes were moving underneath the lids) to the cutting edge. Laced with madcap anecdotes, profound speculation, and common sense, The Sleepwatchers is a door to understanding the mysterious phenomenon called sleep, and a window into a brilliant scientist's mind.

The
SLEEPWATCHERS

William C. Dement, M.D., Ph.D.

Former Chairman,
National Commission on
Sleep Disorders Research

Published by
Nychthemeron Press

Published by Nychthemeron Press
A division of Sleep Disorders Foundation, Inc.
P. O. Box 912, Menlo Park, CA 94026-0912

Library of Congress Catalog Card Number: 96-68413
ISBN: 0-9649338-0-2
(previously published by the Stanford Alumni Association,
ISBN 0-916318-48-6)

10 9 8 7 6 5 4 3

Printed in the United States of America

About the Author

If there was ever someone singularly qualified to write a book on sleep and sleep research, it is Dr. William C. Dement, one of the world's foremost authorities on the subject. In the words of a recent citation from the National Institutes of Health: "Dr. Dement, more than any other individual, is responsible for the creation of a modern, viable field of sleep research, especially as it relates to sleep-related pathologies."

Dr. Dement is the former chairman of the National Commission on Sleep Disorders Research, a position to which he was appointed in 1990. In 1961, he co-founded the Sleep Research Society; in 1975, he founded the American Sleep Disorders Association, serving as its president for twelve years. In addition to such activist roles, Dr. Dement has been honored for his work by so many organizations—the National Institute on Aging, American Psychiatric Association, American Association for the Advancement of Science, and American Medical Association, to name just a few—that to list them would fill this page and more. Among the more than 400 scientific publications he has authored or co-authored are the still-popular Portable Stanford volume *Some Must Watch While Some Must Sleep*, published in 1972, and the medical textbook *Principles and Practices of Sleep Medicine* (1989). Withal, he maintains a strong interest in teaching; his courses on sleep and dreams at Stanford have attracted upwards of 500 undergraduates per class.

Dr. Dement was raised in Walla Walla, Washington. After receiving his B.S. from the University of Washington in 1951, he left for the University of Chicago, where he earned his M.D. in 1955 and his Ph.D. in neurophysiology in 1957. In 1963 he came to the Stanford University School of Medicine to become director of that institution's Sleep Research Laboratory. Since then he has conducted research on basic and clinical aspects of sleep, including the functional significance of the different sleep states. Today he is the Lowell W. and Josephine Q. Berry Professor of Psychiatry and Behavioral Sciences at Stanford, as well as director of the Stanford Sleep Research Center—the world's first such facility, which he founded in 1970. Currently, Dr. Dement's group is focusing on the basic control mechanisms of the sleep/wakefulness cycle, such as the biological clock, a tiny portion of the brain that controls all of the body's rhythmic processes—including, of course, sleep.

Dr. Dement is married and has three children and two grandsons. In his spare time—no kidding—he enjoys fine wine and gourmet cuisine and loves to play bridge and croquet, although he lacks outstanding expertise at either.

Second Edition

Project Manager: Marvin T. Miles
First Assistant to Project Manager: Ellen Lanzone
Second Assistant to Project Manager: Jan Klein
Supervising Editor: Molly Haselhorst
Editor: Susan Wise
Layout: Molly Haselhorst
Production Manager: Becky Morris
Cover Design: Renée Kollias, Becky Morris
Cover Illustration: Tim Lewis
Back Cover Photograph: Randy Silver

First Edition

Editor-in-Chief: Della van Heyst
Series Editor and Manager: Bruce Goldman
Manuscript Editor: Beverly Cory

Contents

Chapter 1

Chapter 2

Chapter 3

Chapter 4

Making It Through the Night   *57*

Chapter 5

The Circadian Rhythm of Sleep   *81*

Chapter 6

Chapter 7

Chapter 8

Chapter 9

Preface to the 1995 Reissue

Although we are entering the era of the "Information Highway," we are also in the age of "information anxiety," and "input overload." Many people don't seem to want more information, particularly if it is delivered in a dry textbook format. Several recent books on sleep more or less appropriate for the general public have not sold very well.

The Sleepwatchers may have been an exception. Originally written in response to a request from the Stanford University Alumni Association for a small book on sleep targeted toward the "intelligent layperson," all copies of the book were sold in slightly more than a year and it is no longer available. The rapid sales plus a number of favorable comments have suggested that it is, indeed, easy to read and entertaining as well. In addition, during the period that it has been out of print, there has been no letup in requests to obtain additional copies.

For these reasons, I have decided *The Sleepwatchers* should be reissued. As with the original offering to Stanford Alumni, it is my hope that a little "light reading," which also conveys the essential facts of sleep and sleep disorders, will help fill the "vast reservoir of ignorance" about sleep in our society.

Although my original intent was simply to reissue the volume with no changes, upon reflection, this was not possible. Too much has happened that should be communicated. I have, therefore, also taken advantage of this opportunity to add an "update" chapter to relate advances that have taken place in the intervening four years since the original Portable Stanford edition appeared. In 1993, research was published that established the national prevalence of one specific sleep disorder, obstructive sleep apnea. It is much more common than previously thought. For this reason, I urge readers particularly to study Chapter 10 which addresses this and other advances. Finally, I have also reworked the Introduction to make it more appropriate to non-Stanford readers. All other chapters are, for all intents and purposes, identical with those in the 1992 edition. I have only smoothed out no more than ten awkward sentences. I hope readers will not be skeptical about this latter statement as they go through the book.

William C. Dement
Stanford University
December, 1995

Preface to the
1992 Portable Stanford
Edition

Nearly twenty years ago, in 1972, I published a book through the Stanford Alumni Association, called *Some Must Watch While Some Must Sleep,* with the aim of conveying to the general public some of the exciting things I had learned in my twenty years of research into sleep and dreams. As years passed and the volume became increasingly dated, I came to regard it in ever more slighting terms. This devaluation reached a climax in 1983, one of many years during which I was very involved in football recruiting for the Stanford athletic program. Some of the high-school athletes that came to the campus each January were interested in my sleep research, and I always blithely gave them an autographed copy of *Some Must Watch While Some Must Sleep.*

Alas, there came a year when a National Collegiate Athletic Association investigator randomly asked a high-school recruit whether he had received any gifts–an NCAA no-no– while at Stanford. The affirmative reply triggered a full-scale investigation of the Stanford recruiting program. It was clean, except for me–I had given this and other high-school football players *books*, heaven forbid.   To clear the football program and to avoid penalties like being barred from television appearances, I had to sign an affidavit that my book had no value whatsoever. Has any professor ever made a greater personal sacrifice for their University?

The fact is, of course, that my original volume is not up-to-date on the new knowledge about sleep, wakefulness, and circadian rhythms that has been accumulated in the past two decades. This book is an attempt to fill in some of the many holes, as well as to tell the story of sleep research through the eyes of one who has been immersed in the field practically from the start. It also reflects the continuing effort to zoom in on what every human being or man, woman and child should know about sleep and its impact on wakefulness.

Sleep research at Stanford University has been on the world stage for a very long time. The likely reason for this high visibility is that all mankind has an interest in sleep and its problems, yet only a few places have consistently attempted to shed light on its mysteries. I have been at Stanford University since January 1963 and have worked unremittingly and intensely on sleep and its disorders with a host of talented colleagues, some of whom have been fortunate enough to have started sleep research programs elsewhere.

One feature of my tenure at Stanford that has meant a lot to me has been my involvement with undergraduate education. Through my teaching I have gained access to a tremendous supply of undergraduates who wanted to participate in sleep research. The degree to which Stanford undergraduates have participated in and contributed to the knowledge base of the field of sleep research and sleep disorders medicine may be unprecedented. Some of these students have even devised their own experiments, which ultimately led to advances in the field.

As a final caveat, there are times when I believe I sound as if I have retired. This could not be further from the truth. The sleep program at Stanford is in its most exciting and productive phase, and I am surrounded by extremely able scientific colleagues and an unusually gifted administrative staff, which makes everything–research, teaching, and patient care–possible.

It will be obvious to all that this book is highly selective, mainly due to page constraints, and also very personal, so that many exciting and worthy experiments by sleep researchers elsewhere are not mentioned. If I were to mention everyone whose work has guided mine, or who has joined me in organizational and political efforts, it might add up to 1,000 names. In order not to slight anyone, I just want to express my hope that everyone knows how grateful I am for their colleagueship and support. I have enjoyed working with the Stanford Alumni Association, particularly with Bruce Goldman and Amy Pilkington. Bruce is amazing in his various abilities, especially the ability to move things along.

In recent years a shadow has fallen over the life of my daughter Elizabeth and, therefore, over our whole family. Her courage and persistence has been an inspiration. Most of all, this book is for her.

William C. Dement
Stanford University
December, 1991

After All, It's Only One-Third of Your Life

As I write this introduction, an amazing paradox exists in our society. In recent years, we have learned that pervasive sleep deprivation and undiagnosed sleep disorders are arguably our largest health problem. A single sleep problem, obstructive sleep apnea, is now known by sleep researchers to afflict 30 million people. If unrecognized in its advanced stages, this disorder is disabling and eventually lethal. If recognized and treated, even those who are near death's door can be saved and restored to normal health. Effective treatments and cures for many other serious sleep disorders have been developed and are readily available. A huge amount of scientific and clinical knowledge has been rapidly accumulated by dedicated sleep specialists. The paradox is that our society does not know these things. The benefits of hard earned knowledge about normal and pathological sleep have not been passed on to the general public and practicing physicians. Millions of people are suffering and dying without ever knowing the true cause of their troubles. There is almost no teaching about sleep disorders in American medical schools. Teaching about sleep and dreams, the nature and consequences of sleep deprivation, and common sleep disorder symptoms is absent from our universities and colleges. Perhaps the saddest omission of all is that student drivers learn nothing about the dangers of driving drowsy in their training programs, and an astounding number soon die because they fall asleep at the wheel.

This paradox is all the more difficult to understand when we acknowledge that sleep *is* a primary function of our brains, occupying nearly a third of its activity each day and strongly affecting us during the remaining (waking) two-thirds of the day.

So why do most of us continue to be so ignorant about sleep? Here is my explanation. In the first half of this century, sleep was not generally regarded as worthy of study. It was regarded as a "short death," the brain turned off. Even today, many of us continue to look at sleep merely as a turning off, a tuning out of our waking consciousness. Many people experience sleep as a gap—they close their eyes, they open them, and eight hours have passed. Other people experience sleep as fitful and interrupted; they are aware of things going on, but nowhere, they would say, near the level of wakefulness.

The stereotype that continues to dominate human thinking about sleep is that it comes when the brain is shutting down—indeed, that sleep itself is nothing more complicated than the brain shut down. Ask almost anyone whether the brain is more active during wakefulness or during sleep, and they would surely say wakefulness.

Dreaming, the lone exception to this stereotype, is regarded as fleeting and ephemeral, sometimes associated with partial arousals. Indeed, even Freud thought that dreams occurred only in response to such partial arousals, to deal with disturbing stimuli–in other words, to protect sleep. So, according to this ingrained and pervasive stereotype, going to sleep means putting the car in the garage and turning off the ignition. There is nothing interesting going on. There is no likelihood of a breakdown, and there is nothing worth studying other than how not to wake up. Right? No, wrong, absolutely wrong.

The exact opposite is true. The brain in sleep, this marvelous organ, is an *active* brain; it no more shuts off when we fall asleep than the liver or the pancreas or the lungs. In fact, in the mode of sleep called REM sleep, brain activity revs up to levels equal to or greater than those attained in the waking state. Today it is possible to image the normal living human brain, and the information on brain activity during sleep that was obtained years ago from experimental animals has been solidly confirmed in all its essentials.

As recently as 1980 we could say that the practice of medicine ended when the patient fell asleep. As I will relate, at Stanford we realized that this was a grotesque error as early as 1972. We realized that an enormous number of medical disorders were specifically related to the sleeping brain, not the waking brain. However, by this time the clinical community and medical education system had organized itself into a number of subspecialties with rigid boundaries and was also experiencing a need to contain costs. Therefore, easy and rapid growth of a new and entirely unique clinical enterprise was no longer possible. Consequently, the diagnosis and treatment of sleep disorders has never penetrated the medical education system, and there was no public mandate for education and research that might have energized an expansion of education and awareness in other components of our society.

As a result of my work on the Congressionally mandated National Commission on Sleep Disorders Research from 1990 to 1992 and the activities I undertook in an effort to foster the implementation of its recommendations, I am now firmly convinced that pervasive sleep deprivation and undiagnosed, misdiagnosed and mistreated sleep disorders are collectively America's largest, deadliest, and most costly health problem. The Commission found unaddressed problems involving sleep in every component of society. For many years, sleep specialists have been able to diagnose and treat a number of serious sleep disorders. Yet, millions of people are suffering and dying needlessly, because health professionals remain almost completely unaware. In spite of this, we find that there is no curriculum for sleep disorders in American medical schools. This is an omission which must be remedied as soon as possible, but it is also necessary to teach busy practicing physicians to recognize at least some sleep disorders and to encourage the victims to complain about them.

The stereotype of the brain turned off has also delayed the human race from discovering the secrets of sleep. At this point, we simply do not know what the sleeping brain is doing and why it is doing it, at least not in the same way we know what the waking brain is doing and why. When we are awake, the major task of our brain is to orchestrate our behavior in the world. This requires learning, remembering, moving about, projecting ourselves into the future, planning—all those things that concern our interactions with our external environment in the service of our survival as individuals and as a species.

The Task or Tasks of the Active Sleeping Brain Must Be Totally Different from the Waking Brain

One of the major ecological aspects of sleep is that the internal drive to sleep and the cues that the time to sleep is coming—sunset and so forth—remind the organism to seek its particular safe place: for birds or monkeys, a perch high in a tree; for other animals, a den, a tunnel, or a cave. For certain animals who are quite safe because of their strength and ferocity, no such need exists. Thus, lions sleep anywhere, any time.

But why do lions sleep at all? Why do *all* species sleep? Why is sleep so peremptory? Why does it overtake us, even under circumstances when nodding off might threaten our very lives? The reason must be that the brain has something else to do—or many things to do—that cannot be done when its neural circuitry is preoccupied with sensing and responding to the environment. It seems highly likely that the functions and tasks of the brain in sleep relate to maintenance of the organism in ways we do not fully understand. Furthermore, it would be absurd to hypothesize that the brain in sleep performs but a single task.

For all of us, then, the proper view of sleep is that waking consciousness temporarily ends and another kind of consciousness takes over. Sleep is the twin sibling of wakefulness, a valued companion with a full-fledged existence. The giving up of waking consciousness might be akin to watching an airplane taking off. The airplane is not shutting itself down; it is going elsewhere, and our waking consciousness cannot follow. Of course, this metaphor is not perfect; if we pay attention, we do have limited access to our sleeping thoughts and our dreams.

My sincerest hope is that those who read this book will give up the "shutting down" stereotype—will come to think of sleep merely as a different activity—and, when lying in bed at night, will feel themselves taking off into the realm of sleep as opposed to shutting down. If I am successful, then the established metaphors will be revised. Falling asleep no longer will be regarded as a process of going through the house and turning off all the lights, but rather of flipping the switch from visible light to ultraviolet or infrared. In fact, the ideal way to state this fact is "the brain never sleeps!" The body sleeps, but the brain never sleeps.

Having been at Stanford since 1963, I have enjoyed the profound experience of teaching a steady stream of undergraduates. One aspect of teaching an introductory course to undergraduates is that it moves a specialist much closer to a more simple and clear teaching mode. At first, I had a great deal of trouble reaching the right mix of simplicity, clarity, and communicating an understanding of relatively complex phenomena. In addition, I became very impressed at how little specific course content students remembered a year or so later. Because of the importance of the material, and because it would very likely be the students' only exposure in their entire lives, I wanted to present the material in my course on sleep and dreams in a way that the students would remember certain facts for their entire lives.

With regard to the latter aim, I have been strongly influenced by a book that is even slimmer than this one, entitled *1066 and All That*, written in 1931 by the English historians, W.C. Sellar and R.J. Yeatman. At this point, I cannot resist repeating an anecdote that became a traditional part of the introductory lecture to the more than eight hundred undergraduates in my annual course on sleep and dreams. Sellar and Yeatman firmly state that "history is what you can remember." They claim that the average Englishman can remember only two dates in history, one of which is always the Battle of Hastings. The first time I taught the sleep and dreams course, I described this remarkable thesis on history and memory and suggested to the students that if the average Englishman could remember little more history than the date 1066, I could hardly expect them to remember the myriad details contained in thousands of publications on sleep and dreams. I would therefore, I said, undertake a somewhat different pedagogic style and emphasize principles, particularly "A Few Important Principles," that I would expect them to remember for the remainder of their lives. I further suggested that although a future *Memorable Introduction to Sleep Research* might be a very slim volume, we would all know what was in it.

Throughout the ensuing semester, I verbally underscored the facts and principles that the students "should always remember," such as "there are two entirely different kinds of sleep and their names are REM and NREM," "good health must include healthy sleep," and so forth. At the end of the semester, well satisfied with myself and my pedagogic philosophy, I gave a multiple-choice examination, except, for the last question, I asked, "write one thing from the course that you will surely remember for the rest of your life." Nearly all the students wrote "1066." To this day, I am not sure whether they were telling me something very profound about the educational process, or whether their response was just an extremely well-executed put-on. For about ten years, I started the course by telling this story, but haven't recently. I used to run into alumni from the course all over the world. They would almost always greet me with the words, "1066."

Recently, I experienced an amazing moment, a pause, almost an epiphany. I had just finished what I believe was a fairly stimulating talk about sleep and dreams and sleep disorders to a group of individuals at a health spa. Very few were health professionals, but all were, of course, interested in good health. At the end of my talk, someone raised a hand and said, "Can you suggest a good book on sleep and sleep disorders for the layman?" I cannot explain why this caught me completely off guard, yet it did. Richard Harter, a sleep technician who had driven me to the health spa, and I looked at each other questioningly. There followed, in fact, a long silence. Finally, I said, somewhat hesitantly, "I am embarrassed to tell you, a really good book for the layman does not exist."

Although I have intended to write such a book, and to make it fairly authoritative and comprehensive, as of this moment I have not begun this task, and it will presumably take a fair amount of time. In the aftermath of that watershed question in the health spa, I resolved that something must be done immediately. It is no longer acceptable to be unable to respond to such requests. It is no longer acceptable to stimulate listeners and have nothing further to offer them to satisfy the curiosity and interest that have been aroused. Finally, how can the sleep community continue to rail about the lack of public awareness when there is no book about sleep that can be enthusiastically recommended for the general reader.

As a matter of fact, I have written two books, more or less for the general public. Both of these books were written as part of the Stanford University Alumni Association's "Portable Stanford" series. Both were "sold out." The first was published 23 years ago, in 1972, and was called *Some Must Watch While Some Must Sleep*. This book, of course, does not contain the new knowledge about sleep, wakefulness, and circadian rhythms that has been accumulated since it was published more than two decades ago. The second book, *Sleepwatchers*, published in 1992 was an attempt to fill in new knowledge, as well as to tell the story of sleep research through the eyes of one who has been immersed in the field practically from the start. It also reflected the continuing effort to zoom in on what every human being or man, woman and child should know about sleep and its impact on their daily lives.

It is high time for sleepwatchers to make a major commitment to educate the general public. At the very least, we certainly must not stand dumbfounded if someone asks for more information or a book on the subject. It is for this reason that I have decided to reissue the second Portable Stanford volume, *The Sleepwatchers*, and to update it slightly. By so doing, I can make something immediately available, at least for my own use to cite after lectures, and can meet the demand while I or someone else prepare something a little more comprehensive.

To be quite honest, it feels like a major challenge to write a book about sleep that people will want to read. I can understand someone experiencing such a desire after an interesting lecture, but a general desire to seek a book on sleep with the same eagerness as one would pursue a spine-tingling adventure thriller is something we probably could not inspire in people. However, there is for some people a subtle sense of awe and mystery surrounding the "short death" we call sleep, and they wonder about the journey through the night. Certainly, in primitive times, human beings wondered about the long period of nocturnal immobility during which the life force seemed to leave the body, and during which the soul seemed to travel abroad.

Driving late one very cloudy night in the back country east of Lake Tahoe years ago, my thoughts drifted to this problem. I tried to comprehend the unimaginable gulf between the present and life some million years ago, before man could control fire. How unthinkingly we accept our cities, electric lights, automobiles, our technological miracles! I tried to recall if I had ever been away from all this, somewhere in total darkness where I would have experienced the solitude that must have been known to our distant ancestors. As I mused, I realized that I might be in such a place at that very moment. On an impulse, I turned off the blacktop onto a dirt road and drove perhaps five miles along this winding path. There was no moon, no stars; but for the headlights of my car picking up bits of reality in the vast spread of darkness, I would have felt totally suspended in time and space.

At a wide place in the road, I stopped the car, turned off the lights and the motor, and got out. My hand could feel the cold metal of the car, but I could see nothing. I had walked only a few paces when a wave of apprehension enveloped me. Suppose I got lost? Suppose I became disoriented and could not find my way back to the car? My foreboding increased with each additional step until, in a surge of panic, I turned and started back. But where was the car? How far had I come? Now the utter darkness, the pitch blackness of the night, filled me with a kind of primordial dread and horror. Groping and stumbling, I managed to locate the car before I became entirely paralyzed by fright. As I climbed back into my warm, safe, familiar automobile, I realized with new insight that night was once man's enemy. The sleep process carried with it a gentle protection from the psychic terrors spawned in the long hours of unrelieved blackness.

Perhaps family life itself originated from the need to sleep and to cluster for protection while in this state. Because sleep occurs during the dark hours when man is least able to cope with his environment, and because man asleep is not alert to the dangers of the outer world, sleep is a state of vulnerability. It is necessary to seek a place of refuge in which to sleep. A troop of baboons has its tree, the wolf has its den, primitive man had his cave or his hut, and we have our bedrooms. Having constructed a safe place to sleep, man is able to use the word "home."

On the lighter side, sleep has also manifested an economic effect in paraphernalia ranging from pillows and pajamas to eiderdown sleeping bags and campers on wheels. Consider the bed. From a simple animal hide or a pile of leaves on a dirt floor, the bed has grown to a box spring and mattress, and now to a water-filled balloon; twin-size, double, queen, king, and room-size; rectangular, square, heart-shaped, or amorphous. The business of lodging travelers has grown from the scattered wayside inns of medieval Europe to thousands of hotels and motels all over the world.

On a more personal note, I have been a sleep specialist and nothing else my entire professional career and even before that as a medical student. I have been around for the entirety of what has been called the "modern era of sleep research" ushered in by the discovery of rapid eye movements during sleep in 1952. (I will say more about this discovery in Chapter 2.) Back in the 1950s, I certainly did not expect that I would be able to earn a living by doing research on sleep and dreams. However, I had the good luck to obtain a research fellowship stipend from the United States Public Health Service when I graduated from medical school in 1955. At the time, $3000 a year for two years to do exactly what I wanted seemed almost unbelievable. Although I am not the first person to devote his entire career to the study of sleep, I am surely the first person in the history of the world whose salary was always specifically paid for studying sleep. I really didn't do it for the money. I did it for love. I have been endlessly delighted and fascinated by the discoveries made by me and by the growing number of students and colleagues over the years. I have been rewarded by ever increasing understanding of the role of sleep in our lives, and I have been privileged to share this knowledge and understanding as much as possible with students, colleagues, practicing physicians, and people everywhere.

All of the foregoing may be interesting, and subsets of this vast field may be particularly fascinating to one person or another. There are, however, two main areas where our sleep clearly has great significance for the lives and health of each and every one of us, and collectively for the health of our nation and the entire world. The first is simple and obvious. Alert, energetic wakefulness during the day requires adequate, healthy sleep at night. The second is more complex and constitutes the content of a relatively new medical specialty, sleep medicine, which involves the diagnosis and treatment of a host of specific sleep disorders, at least one of which we will all eventually experience. Sleep and its disorders has and will have a major impact upon our existence and we should therefore know something about it. The facts we can discuss are fascinating in themselves; but more than that, they are crucial to each reader's health and longevity. Our society needs to assign a higher priority to discovering more about this uncharted path of our existence, these other states of being. We must come to think of this unexplained phenomenon as an equal partner in the triumvirate of health: proper nutrition, physical fitness, and good, healthy sleep.

1

Wake Up America!

On March 24, 1989, the giant oil tanker Exxon Valdez slammed into Bligh Reef off the coast of Alaska in Prince William Sound. Two hundred fifty-eight thousand barrels of crude oil spilled onto one of the most beautiful unspoiled coastlines in the world. The environmental damage of this catastrophe will never be accurately assessed, but the cost of the subsequent clean-up effort was estimated at about $2 billion. In a July 1990 report, the National Transportation Safety Board identified the primary cause of the accident as the third mate's failure to maneuver the vessel properly. The description of the third mate's behavior on the bridge minutes before the accident is both sad and dramatic: He was simply so sleepy he could not perform.

Another report from the National Transportation Safety Board describes its painstaking investigation of 278 fatal-to-the-driver truck accidents. The Board identifies the major cause of such fatalities as sleep deprivation and fatigue—an even greater hazard than drugs and alcohol.

These findings hint at a mammoth but camouflaged societal problem: America is a nation whose citizens do not get enough sleep. At a public meeting of the National Commission on Sleep Disorders Research in November 1990, Dr. Norman Edelman, dean of the Robert Wood Johnson School of Medicine, summed it up: "America is a sleep-deprived society, and [that condition] is interfering with its societal mission."

The problem is so pervasive that it is not clearly perceived. Moreover, the known facts about how, and to what degree, sleep loss impedes waking performance are not presented at any educational level—not in middle-school health education classes, not in high-school or college biology or psychology classes, not even, for the most part, in medical school. We have pinpointed chronic sleep deprivation and inadequate sleep as one of America's greatest health issues, causing problems in the workplace, in the classroom, and at home; yet, this knowledge is unavailable to the public. As a result, the way Americans conduct their lives and organize their work and rest schedules remains irrational and destructive.

Another chilling example of the high cost of sleepiness was the disaster involving the space shuttle *Challenger*, in which seven astronauts were blown up in front of 50 million television viewers, including millions of children. An investigation of this disaster by a special Presidential body called the Rogers Commission spotlighted faulty O-rings, but also implicated the work/rest schedules of key managers who made the erroneous decision to go ahead with the launch. Two of the top three NASA managers had obtained less than three hours of sleep apiece for three consecutive nights before that fatal choice was made on the evening before the launch. My own speculation is that, in their severely sleep-deprived condition, these managers weren't able to assess the full impact of the O-ring data they were receiving from the manufacturer, Morton Thiokol. The *Challenger* accident was catastrophic to the space program; in terms of the actual dollar costs, delays, and lost momentum, the cost must have been in the billions.

Many occupations are associated with sleep loss and excessive sleepiness, which in turn impair both mood and ability to function. In many cases, performance failures on the job can kill, maim, destroy property, and cause far-reaching catastrophes—as happened when night workers failed to respond optimally in the Chernobyl and Three Mile Island nuclear accidents. In addition to such dramatic events, there are thousands of lesser accidents on the highway, in our factories, and at home that do not receive the same publicity, yet may be equally catastrophic to individual lives.

You've seen the stories in the newspapers. A South Dakota man, driving behind a large truck carrying steel girders, remembers he should stop for a cup of coffee. The next thing he knows is that his car has slammed into the rear of the truck stopped at a crossroad, and his wife is on the seat beside him, dead—decapitated when one of the girders smashed through the car's windshield. Or maybe you read the sadly ironic story about the New Hampshire teenager who, in July 1989, received the National Safest Teenage Driver Award. Just seven months later, this 17-year-old was dead, having fallen asleep at the wheel—his car drifted into a head-on collision, also killing the other driver.

"Accidents" of this nature are not accidents; they are the inevitable consequence of inadequate sleep. None of this is necessary. A strategy as trivial as an evening nap might have saved the *Exxon Valdez*. Closer to home, some simple knowledge and understanding of how the urge to sleep can take us by surprise might prevent a young student from getting into a car to drive home from a party or a late night study session—and into a one car rollover.

We have become a 24-hour society, and yet we have not begun to structure our schedules for optimum function. The necessary facts have been gathered through sleep research; they only need to be communicated and understood. Individuals may still choose to risk their lives, but at least they ought to have a choice. Some day, driving or going to work while sleepy will be as reprehensible and even criminally negligent as driving or going to work while drunk.

Science Looks Away

After the Korean War, there was considerable discussion in American Psychiatric circles about whether sleep deprivation could lead to psychosis. The North Koreans had reputedly used sleep deprivation as a technique of extorting confessions from prisoners of war, and a number of anecdotal reports spoke of mental breakdowns under these circumstances. In 1965, a group of Stanford sleepwatchers had the opportunity to observe a young high school student whose aim was to break the world's record for prolonged wakefulness. By staying awake for eleven consecutive days, he exceeded the previous record by 64 hours. At no time during his prolonged vigil did he show any signs of serious mental aberration, certainly not a mental breakdown. After we had confirmed this in several subsequent studies, we theorized that only a minimal amount of sleep was absolutely necessary. When asked about the need for sleep, I would generally reply, "Four hours a night."

I was totally wrong, but in 1965 I was not alone; sleep-watchers had not yet recognized the problems of daytime sleepiness.

Human beings have surely been aware since the dawn of history that they could not get along without sleep, and that there is a direct connection between the lack of sleep and the desire for it. For centuries, though, the universal consequence of reduced or disturbed sleep did not come under anyone's serious scrutiny. The scientific community in general, and sleep researchers in particular, paid absolutely no attention to it until well into the 1970s. As recently as 1982, when I was writing an article on daytime sleepiness, I looked in the indexes of a number of introductory psychology textbooks and could find no mention of the word—no listing in any of them— for *sleepiness, drowsiness,* or even *alertness*; all, needless to say, extremely important qualities of psychological functioning. Nowhere, either in psychology or medical texts, was sleepiness mentioned as a factor in mental performance. But it was only when I discovered the same absence in the index of the monumental monograph in my field—*Sleep and Wakefulness,* written by Nathaniel Kleitman, the trailblazer of modern sleep research—that I realized the true magnitude of science's failure to deal with the issue of daytime sleepiness.

In spite of its remarkable absence from textbooks, I believe that the dimension of sleepiness/alertness—from the moment before sleep, when our minds are completely fogged, all the way to total alertness—is the most important in all of psychology. For twenty years I have been engaged in the sort of research that might eventually get this dimension into the textbooks where it belongs.

The degree of impaired alertness—daytime sleepiness— that exists among individuals and in society as a whole should concern us all. That such an epidemic could have been so steadfastly ignored for so long is especially amazing because, like most people, sleepwatchers don't enjoy working at night any more than anyone else does—and here was something they could have studied in the daytime!

The Road to Understanding Sleepiness

Almost everything our field knows about the fundamental determinants of daytime sleepiness was developed and discovered in a Stanford University research facility that we called the Stanford Summer Sleep Camp. The camp director over its entire span of ten years, from 1976 to 1985, was Mary Carskadon, who is now a full professor at E.P. Bradley Hospital at Brown University. The camp was housed from June through the early days of September in the Lambda Nu fraternity house at the edge of Lake Lagunita (which, incidentally, dries up each summer, giving a somewhat less recreational air to the quasi-camp environment). The "camp counselors" were almost entirely Stanford undergraduates whom we trained intensively each spring. Summer after summer, they conducted the kind of painstaking scientific research that may not win a Nobel Prize but is, nonetheless, of supreme importance. The application of this research is likely to save untold thousands if not millions of lives. (The proportion of Sleep Camp counselors who went on to careers in medicine and science is phenomenal.)

The direct scientific attack on daytime sleepiness in the Stanford Summer Sleep Camp would not have come about were it not for the clinical problems we were seeing on a daily basis in the Stanford University Sleep Disorders Clinic, of which I was then director. Our initial interest was in patients diagnosed as having *narcolepsy*, an illness typified by irresistible attacks of sleep, and in those with *sleep apnea syndrome*, a condition of transient but severely disturbing respiratory failure during sleep. Both of these conditions impair daytime alertness. When we first began studying them, though, we had no objective way to measure sleepiness.

Today, we have such a measure—a standardized method called the Multiple Sleep Latency Test (MSLT) that is used all over the world to objectively measure sleepiness. During the spring of 1976, a group of Stanford students carried out the first study of daytime alertness under conditions of total sleep loss. This experiment helped set the ground rules of what would become the MSLT. The students stayed awake for two days, during which time a "sleep latency" measurement was taken every two hours as follows: The student was told to lie quietly in bed, in a darkened room, and to try to fall asleep. As soon as the subject fell asleep, the test was ended—that is, the student was roused—and "sleep latency" was scored according to how many minutes had elapsed (a score of 0 indicating maximum sleepiness; a score of 20 maximum alertness). If the student failed to fall asleep within twenty minutes, the test was ended and the student scored 20. With this test design, no sleep time was permitted to accumulate during the experiment, and the subject did not get too bored if unable to fall asleep. (Sleep latency was also measured before the experiment and again after the subject was finally permitted to sleep.)

During the first night of the experiment, the sleep latency scores dropped essentially to 0—maximum sleepiness— and stayed there for the remainder of the two days. Impressed with the test's results, we tried it over at the Sleep Disorders Clinic, administering it to patients with narcolepsy and to a group of normal volunteers. The patients with narcolepsy had sleep latencies between 0 and 5 minutes on every single test, while the control group usually scored above 10. We found similar values (0-5) in another group of patients with sleep apnea (discussed further in Chapter 4), who were also unable to stay awake. We therefore considered a mean value between 0 and 5 to indicate "pathological" sleepiness. (Of course, values in this range can also occur in normal people simply as a result of sleep deprivation. The difference is that getting more sleep does not relieve the sleepiness in patients with narcolepsy or sleep apnea, while it does in normal individuals.) The test clearly worked; it had given a 100 percent accurate diagnosis of pathological sleepiness in the patient group. Thus the MSLT almost instantly became a staple of sleep disorders medicine, which it remains today.

A Whole Country of Sleepy People

The MSLT was a standard procedure by the time Mary Carskadon and I, with our undergraduate technicians, launched the Stanford Summer Sleep Camp. During ten remarkable summers, we studied sleep patterns and daytime alertness in people of all ages, all of whom spent anywhere from several days to several weeks at the "camp." In one early study, Stanford undergraduate volunteers, given the MSLT on each of several consecutive days, were found to be pathologically sleepy (their sleep latencies were below five minutes) even though they were spending their normal eight hours in bed. When their bedtime was extended to ten hours (with about 9 1/2 hours of actual sleep), their daytime alertness improved. The cause of the severe sleepiness in the undergraduates was obvious: *They simply were not getting enough sleep.* Meanwhile, we were finding that 10-,11-, and 12-year-old children who spent ten hours in bed at night had optimal physiological and subjective alertness in the daytime.

In the summer of 1976 we started what I regard as one of the monumental scientific studies in the area of sleep research. We recruited 24 prepubertal children, ages 10, 11, and 12, for a study that would last ten years and would map the need for sleep across the second decade of life. Although some subjects dropped out along the way, others were added from time to time, and many returned every summer to our Sleep Camp for the standardized studies of their sleep and daytime alertness. Their bedtimes for three to five consecutive nights were 10pm to 8am. During each day we gave the Multiple Sleep Latency Test to establish their level of daytime alertness. With about 9 1/2 hours of sleep, all the prepubertal children were optimally alert, with MSLT scores at or very near 20 (that is, they consistently remained awake for the twenty-minute testing period).

The surprise was that as the subjects grew older and reached puberty, they needed even more sleep. As physically mature 16- to 18-year-olds, they showed significantly impaired daytime alertness with the same 9 1/2 hours of sleep that had served them well at age 10. The study showed clearly that the need for sleep *increases* across the second decade—yet we know from questionnaire studies that most high school students spend no more than seven hours in bed at night. We concluded that high school and college students need much more sleep—two or three hours more every day—than they routinely get.

In another important Sleep Camp study, we partially sleep-deprived ten young adults for seven consecutive nights, allowing them just five hours sleep per night. Over the seven day period, their daytime alertness progressively *worsened*—a result that has been confirmed numerous times by other investigators.

In other words, there is a "sleep debt" that accumulates just like any credit account. The brain keeps very accurate figures on the accruing sleep deficit, which drives the tendency of the brain to fall asleep. The amount of sleep debt that's been built up is what determines the likelihood that any person operating hazardous equipment or making crucial decisions will make a disastrous error.

Since several other groups of investigators, using the MSLT, have also found a severe physiological sleepiness pervasive in communities and in workplace environments, you might expect more people to complain of general fatigue. But people have a strange inability to accurately perceive their sleepiness. Dr. Thomas Roth and his colleagues at Henry Ford Hospital's Sleep Disorders Center (one of the most outstanding) in Detroit reported in 1988 on a study of a large sample of young adults. The subjects were recruited specifically because of their claims that they were *not* bothered by daytime sleepiness or any other health problem. Yet when their daytime alertness was evaluated after eight hours in bed, *40 percent tested pathologically sleepy!* Only about 10 percent of those who claimed to be feeling fine were in fact optimally alert. Almost certainly, of all the individuals who actually *admitted* experiencing daytime sleepiness, a much higher percentage would exhibit sleepiness at the pathological level.

While sleep/wake issues affect myriad public policy areas, there is an unfortunate tendency for uninformed policy makers to suggest that it is "normal" to be sleepy. To test this, Dr. Roth and his colleagues selected a group of the sleepiest subjects and persuaded them to spend ten hours in bed for six consecutive nights. Just as we had found in the Stanford Summer Sleep Camp, ten hours of sleep improved their daytime alertness significantly. Furthermore, their ability to perform intellectually also improved! Thus, the intellectual capacity of these sleepy individuals, who thought they were in great shape, had actually been significantly impaired. If feeling this way is the "norm," then we are unquestionably a sleep-deprived and suboptimal society. Nearly all of us need more sleep than we get.

The Crisis in Awareness

It's clear from the research that much chronic daytime sleepiness results from simply not enough hours in bed—

but that's only part of America's problem. Such sleepiness can also arise from sleep disorders of various sorts, disorders that are quite prevalent in the population but go largely unrecognized by the public and general medical profession alike. The popular press has lately latched on to some of the problems: *Prevention* magazine in November 1990 ran a "Snore-Score Questionnaire" designed to alert readers to possible sleep apnea; and *TIME* magazine's December 17, 1990 cover story, "The Sleep Gap: Too Much to Do, Too Little Rest," deplored the widespread sleepiness in American society and its devastating implications. Yet in spite of this apparent growth in awareness, there is a persistent lack of practical response.

After two decades, sleep disorders medicine is now an accredited clinical specialty in the United States, with well over 200 fully accredited sleep disorders centers nationwide. Nevertheless, throughout the medical profession as a whole, attention to the facts of sleep remains at an extremely low level. In 1979, Stanford sleep specialists did a study of local primary care and family practice physicians, interviewing patients and checking their medical records. We found that up to 50 percent of the patients had serious sleep complaints when we interviewed them, yet only about 2 percent of these complaints had been noted by the primary care physicians. A number of continuing medical education exercises in the ensuing decade, designed to increase family physicians' awareness of the importance of sleep, appear to have wrought no significant change.

If anything, there has been absolutely no improvement in the last decade. The advent of computerized records and standardized clinical terminology has enabled us to scan large medical groups' records on over 10 million patients. We recently found diagnosis of the common (but serious) sleep disorder we call "obstructive sleep apnea" in only 97 patients, or less that 0.0001 percent of all cases—an infinitesimal number, considering that we should have seen an absolute minimum of 100,000 such diagnoses in a patient population of this size. In a follow-up to the 1979 study, we scrutinized more than 10,000 charts in primary-care practices around the San Francisco Bay Area and found fewer than 1 percent with any notation at all about sleep.

Even when doctors *do* note sleep problems, the physician's response often has no rational basis. For example, an obese patient with high blood pressure, cacophonous snoring, and excessive daytime sleepiness—sure signs of obstructive sleep apnea—was given a benzodiazepine because the doctor wrongly thought depression was a cause of excessive sleepiness. In another probe, we asked about twenty patients from our Sleep Disorders Clinic, all with specifically diagnosed disorders, to take their complaints to primary care doctors to see what would happen. In not one instance was there an appropriate response.

This pervasive lack of awareness may be the fault *not* of the primary care physician, but of the specialists who fail to make sleep disorders medicine easy to absorb into the daily routine of primary care physicians who do not have large amounts of time to spend with their patients. In an effort to help with the diagnosis, we have designed a system for asking all the crucial questions in about ten minutes, and we expect it to make a difference.

Meanwhile, of the approximately 10 million estimated victims of sleep apnea in the United States, somewhere around 8 to 9.5 million are still undiagnosed. In other words, for every diagnosed case, over four to twenty people are wandering around with no idea they have this serious problem. Their severe sleepiness constitutes a threat to themselves and to others because of their vulnerability to accidents. Their productivity and ability to learn is profoundly impaired, and their cardiovascular health is threatened. Sleep apnea is relatively easy to diagnose; effective treatments are available. Anyone who has troublesome daytime sleepiness should consider sleep apnea before assuming that the problem is solely a matter of chronic sleep deprivation.

I hope that by the time these words are read, a visit to the family doctor will produce rational and effective results. As a further step, it will be important to incorporate the facts about sleep and common sleep problems into biology and psychology programs, beginning in high school and carrying on through college and medical school. Otherwise, as we see today, more than 95 percent of all sleep problems will remain undiagnosed and untreated. Considering the dangers of sleep deprivation spelled out earlier in this chapter, that constitutes a true societal crisis.

What's Your Sleep-Debt Awareness Quotient?

Over the past several decades, the American public has seen various campaigns by the government and the medical profession, designed to increase awareness of the benefits of sound nutrition and physical fitness. A similar campaign is needed to change people's perception of their need for sleep.

Everyone knows that when you stay awake all night, the chances are that you will experience troublesome drowsiness the following day. However, most people think this is a transient phenomenon, easily reversed and of no serious consequence. They also think that drowsiness is not always related to loss of sleep, and can be caused by such things as a glass of wine, a boring lecture, a warm or stuffy room, or a heavy meal. They don't know about the insidious and unremitting nature of sleep debt.

A thorough understanding of your personal sleep debt and what it means for your life is a challenge, because the reality often differs from what your feelings are telling you. (It's like trying to believe that the world is a round ball when your eye, scanning the horizon, tells you it's flat as a pancake. But even the Society for the Preservation of the Flat Earth finally disbanded in 1970 in the face of the incontrovertible photographic evidence from the Apollo missions that the Earth was truly round.) The fact is, how sleepy you feel at any given moment is not always a reliable assessment of your sleep debt.

Exactly what is sleepiness, and why is it so hard for people to identify it accurately? By the simplest definition, sleepiness denotes a condition that is associated with an increased tendency for a person to fall asleep. It is, in short, a biological drive. The sleep drive is manifested both as an elemental feeling, or *subjective* sleepiness, and as a powerful tendency to fall asleep, or *physiological* sleepiness. Subjective sleepiness and physiological sleepiness are related in the same way that hunger and starvation are related. If you are starving to death, you may or may not feel hungry, depending on the circumstances. You can be distracted and may even forget that you are hungry for a time, but this does not change your physiological state of starvation. On the other hand, if you are satiated with food, you never feel hungry.

By the same token, a sleep-deprived person may or may not feel sleepy at any given moment, depending upon the degree of environmental or internal stimulation. If stimulation is high, a sleep-deprived person can momentarily feel very alert. But the sleep debt is not reduced at all, and the brain remains just as ready to fall asleep. Lowering the level of stimulation—with a boring speaker, a heavy meal, a soothing glass of wine, a warm room, or general quiet—will immediately allow both subjective and physiological sleepiness to reassert themselves. Because this is such a commonplace experience, people think of the factors of reduced stimulation as the *causes* of sleepiness. This is a dangerous misattribution, because it assumes that strong waves of drowsiness are caused by something other than sleep deprivation, and that they will permanently dissipate once the "cause" is removed.

In a recent twist, researchers at the Henry Ford Hospital Sleep Disorders Center have shed new light on the purported sedative effects of alcohol, uncovering a powerful interaction between alcohol and the internal sleep debt. Sleepwatchers Timothy Roehrs, Tom Roth, and their colleagues conducted experiments on groups of subjects with three different sleep schedules:

- In the first group, subjects spent ten hours in bed for seven consecutive nights.

- In the second group, subjects spent eight hours in bed for seven consecutive nights

- In the third group, subjects spent eight hours in bed for five consecutive nights, then five hours in bed for the next two nights (simulating a regular work week followed by a socially active weekend).

On the morning after the seventh night, half the subjects in each group were given the same low dose of alcohol, and the other half received a placebo; daytime sleepiness was measured beginning a short time later. The alcohol induced no additional sleepiness in the ten-hour group; it increased sleepiness only moderately in the eight-hour group, after correcting for the placebo effect. And in the third, somewhat sleep-deprived group, the alcohol induced *severe* levels of sleepiness.

This means that in all accidents linked to alcohol, sleep deprivation plays a powerful role. Evidence is beginning to build up that compounds such as alcohol are not sedatives *per se*; it is a property conferred on them, in a sense, by the sleep debt.

That's why it is so vitally important to be aware of your own sleep debt. You have to remember too, that even with a large sleep debt, you may honestly believe you aren't a bit sleepy, because the drive to sleep can be offset by stimulation. The stimulation may be internal, either from your biological clock (discussed in Chapter 5) or from your muscles when you are active (roughly proportional to the intensity of the exercise); or it may be external—noise, light, excitement, social interaction, and so on.

The internal stimulation from your biological clock periodically wanes, leaving you caught with an unassessed and unopposed sleep debt. If your sleep debt is extremely small, nothing much happens even when stimulation is greatly reduced. If the debt is large, the sudden withdrawal of stimulation will cause an almost immediate dropping off to sleep. The most typical circumstance is a social evening —at this time your biological clock is in an active phase, and you are also receiving considerable intellectual or emotional stimulation. Just when it is time to go home, however, the biological clock phases into a quieter mode. You get behind the wheel of your car, and you are driving down the highway when suddenly overcome with sleepiness. Before you can really think about it and do more than slap your face a few times, you fall asleep. The car hits a tree at fifty miles an hour, and a human chapter is closed.

The only sure way to avoid such calamities is to develop an introspective sensitivity to your personal sleep debt. Obviously you can't give yourself the MSLT, but the following conditions would suggest that your sleep debt is near bankruptcy:

1. You have to rely on a loud alarm clock to get you up in the morning. Getting out of the bed is always a struggle, and sometimes you sleep through the alarm.

2. You experience powerful waves of drowsiness several times a day while in a classroom, a meeting, or a movie theater.

3. You sometimes fall asleep without intending to.

4. Your get-up-and-go has gotten up and gone.

5. A single beer or glass of wine seems to hit you awfully hard.

Dr. Dement's Safety Principles for Everyone

- Sleepiness kills! A nap can save your life.

- Your urge to sleep may be camouflaged, hidden.

- When your sleep debt is large, a sleep attack can occur without warning.

- If you feel drowsy, it is almost too late; a wave of drowsiness is "red alert!"

Mary Carskadon and I once observed subjects around the clock for eight consecutive days. With eight hours in bed every night (11pm to 7am), each subject had some level of daytime sleepiness as measured by the MSLT. For several subjects, this level *did not change* over the eight-day testing period. We may presume that for these people, eight hours was very close to the amount of sleep they needed; they were not making up any sleep and improving their alertness, nor were they losing any sleep and further impairing their alertness. Several subjects showed slight improvement of daytime alertness; for them, eight hours was probably a little more sleep than they needed. At the same time, several subjects seemed to get worse; they apparently needed more than eight hours.

You can run the same sort of test on yourself, even without the MSLT, simply by being aware of how much you have slept each night over the past week or so, and learning through trial and error how much sleep you need to maintain reasonable alertness throughout the waking hours.

Parceling Out the Day's 24 Hours

Society generates enormous pressures upon individuals to spend more hours awake. Data from Japan show a gradual reduction in sleep time over this century, from nine hours a night to fewer than seven. I can attest that Japan is a sleep-deprived society, because I spent a morning in the subway station in Tokyo, watching trains pull in and observing that more than half of all Japanese are asleep on the subway at any given moment. Does it make a difference in ordinary life? We can cope fairly easily with a certain degree of sleep debt; we do not need to be at the optimal level of alertness all the time. But the question is, might what we gain in intellectual performance under optimal alertness more than offset the gain in additional hours when we cut back on our sleep?

Society desperately needs a definitive test of this proposition. It would be nice to run a controlled experiment on an entire college class of some 10,000 students. We could randomly select 5,000 of these to try to spend at least nine hours in bed every night and go about their college lives, while the other 5,000 would live the life of the typical sleep-deprived college student. At the end of the year, we could compare the academic standing of the two groups.

For my own part, it would be a sort of hell on Earth to be sleepy all the time. I have absolutely no question that my performance, my ability to comprehend, my ability to deal with complex material, and my "creative juices" are all marvelously enhanced by sleep. As the day wears on, or if I do not get enough sleep at night, the energetic, creative clarity that is an intellectual joy to me is simply absent.

Often the opportunity to sleep is not entirely under one's control—the new parents with a wakeful baby, the shift worker, the intern in a busy hospital, the pilot who works for an overnight air-express company, the trucker whose income depends on the number of miles logged each day. In almost every case, the possibilities and strategies for coping are far from adequate.

If there is one single rule and strategy we should all adopt, it is this: A sudden wave of drowsiness should be treated almost as seriously as chest pain. It is an urgent

warning that *must not be ignored*—particularly in a potentially hazardous situation, when impaired performance, an
error of inattention, even the briefest dozing off could lead
to accident and catastrophe. The appropriate response is to
get some sleep. Take a nap. Various parts of the world
honor the afternoon siesta; America, too, should become a
napping society. Naps ought to be highly respected rather
than something relegated to the toddler set; a napping person should be perceived as rational and sensible and beautiful.

Wake up, America—the alarm has sounded.

2

The History of
REM Sleep:
An Eye-Witness Account

I am frequently asked how I became a sleep researcher, the implication being that my interests are extremely unusual, if not actually crazy. How did I come by this particular passion for the world of sleep with all its problems and wonders? Looking back down the road I've traveled as a sleepwatcher, I can see both how far we've come and how far we have yet to go.

Forty years ago in September 1951, when I arrived as a student at the University of Chicago School of Medicine, sleep was the farthest thing from my mind. As I traveled by train across the mountains and prairies from Walla Walla to Chicago, I was intent on becoming a psychiatrist. It had never occurred to me—or anyone else—that within a few decades, sleep would be vying for a position on the national research agenda. Sleep research was then still in the backwaters.

Nathaniel Kleitman, who was a professor of physiology at the University of Chicago, was the first and only man in the world at the time who had devoted his entire career to the study of sleep. Why weren't there more? As early as the 1930s, scientists could record brain wave patterns through electroencephalography (EEG), and with some persistence, all-night recordings could have been taken.

What prevented this from happening, I believe, was the mistaken notion that during sleep the brain was turned off. This notion was "confirmed" by slowed EEG rhythms sampled from early in the night, which suggested that the brain was, indeed, idling. So, people concluded, why stay up all night to carry out an endlessly repetitive series of measurements? Even Kleitman himself seemed to regard sleep as second class, as "a periodic, temporary cessation or interruption of the waking state, the latter being the prevalent mode of existence for the healthy adult"—or at least so he described it in the opening of his scholarly, comprehensive monograph *Sleep and Wakefulness*, first written in 1939.

As it turns out, though, I owe my professional career in sleep research and sleep disorders to Professor Kleitman. The neurophysiology course that I was taking as a second-year medical student in September 1952 was interesting but uninspiring until Kleitman took over and began to talk about the higher functions of the central nervous system. At one point in the course of his lectures, he devoted an hour, maybe two, to sleep. For me, those one or two hours in 1952 were pivotal. After the lecture, I went to his office in a gray Gothic building called Abbott Hall and knocked on the door. He opened it about six inches. "Yes?"

Slightly taken aback, I said, "Professor Kleitman, I would like to work in your lab."

"Do you know anything about sleep?" he asked.

"Well, no," I answered.

"Read my book," he said, and closed the door—not exactly a slam.

So I read his book—all 429 beautifully written pages of it—and came back to reapply for the opportunity to work in his lab. At that moment, I probably knew more about sleep than anyone in the world, with the exception of Kleitman himself.

The Discovery I Didn't Make

Of the three people who were present when rapid eye movements during sleep were discovered—Kleitman, Eugene Aserinsky, and me—all are alive as I write this chapter. Kleitman, at 95 years is mentally active as ever, and lives in Santa Monica, California. He is still participating in research as a volunteer subject for a longitudinal study of sleep and breathing. His version of the discovery of rapid eye movements during sleep (later to be termed REM) is different from Aserinsky's, and both differ somewhat from what I think actually happened. In this book, you get my version.

When Kleitman wrote the original edition of *Sleep and Wakefulness*, he emphasized the slow, rolling eye movements seen at the onset of sleep. Because disproportionately large areas of the brain are devoted to eye movements, Kleitman reasoned that the slow movements of the eyes might tell us something about the depth of sleep, and he wondered if similar movements would occur at other times during the sleep cycle. In spring of 1952, Kleitman assigned the task of directly observing the eye movements to Eugene Aserinsky, a graduate student working for his Ph.D. in physiology.

Sitting up through the night and staring at someone else's closed eyelids is about as tedious and difficult a task as the human mind could conceive. (If you don't believe me, just try it.) To simplify the task, Kleitman and Aserinsky first simply document periods of "no movement" versus periods of "movement." Thus, if Aserinsky observed anything during a five-minute interval, he could assign that interval to the "movement" category, and relax. Observing infants (as I did later) was less difficult because they sleep in the daytime; observing adults at night—when the researcher, too, longed to sleep—was almost too difficult. However, Aserinsky and Kleitman came across a much easier way to document eye movements.

The eyeball has a steady, if small, voltage difference from cornea to retina, called the *corneo-retinal potential*. When the eyeballs move, they generate electrical signals that can be amplified by stationary electrodes pasted near the eyes. The amplified signals move pens on a chart recorder called an ink-writing oscillograph—the same technique used to record brain waves.

Aserinsky and Kleitman began to use such an apparatus to observe the slow, rolling eye movements. On night, to their great surprise, a different, much more rapid movement showed up in the eye recording. Because almost any background disturbance could jiggle the pens, the pair initially thought that these "rapid eye movement" potentials were electrical or movement-related artifact, not something really happening to the eyes. Aserinsky then devised a method for the two researchers to test the evidence. By actually walking in and observing the subject's closed eyelids when the signals showed up in the recording, they convinced themselves that this was genuine eye-movement activity.

It turns out that rapid eye movements are very easy to see directly. Any parent with a newborn infant can observe them. Any owner of a dog or cat can easily see the eye movements behind closed lids, and REM sleep can be further identified by the presence of muscular twitching in the sleeping pet. It is amazing, in retrospect, that rapid eye movements during sleep were not discovered hundreds of years earlier, and certainly by the turn of the century, either by doting parents or eagle-eyed pediatricians.

When, in the fall of 1952, I first asked Kleitman if I could work with him, he and Aserinsky were at the point of trying to prove to themselves that the electrical potentials were actually generated by rapid eye movements—in other words, a real phenomenon and not artifact. Thus, I was not involved in the very first observations of eye-movement potentials. But since I was the only one, even as a medical student, who seemed to appreciate the importance of this observation, I have occasionally fantasized about being the very first one to have stumbled upon it. Had I approached Kleitman in the *spring*, I might well have been. That was when students in my medical class were supposed to do research. I was one of the few who, for various reasons, did not; in my case, it was mainly shyness. As a first-year student, I simply could not bring myself to ask a professor if I could work with him, I suppose for fear of being rejected.

Be that as it may, I was plunged into the heart of this groundbreaking research when Kleitman put me to work assisting Aserinsky. Whereas in the past spring, we medical students had been allotted a third to half of our time for research, there was no free time in the fall of 1952. Thus, as a full-time medical student, I was staying up two nights a week to carry out research. It was exhausting, but it was unquestionably what I wanted to do. I was hooked.

Eyes of the Dreamer

No one can prove today who was the first to have the "Aha!" insight that these eye movements we were observing might be related to dreaming. My vote goes to Kleitman, but both he and Aserinsky could have had the thought independently and even more or less simultaneously. In any case, when I entered the laboratory in the fall of 1952, one of my tasks was to awaken subjects at night and ask them if they remembered dreaming. Given the ephemeral nature of dreams, the results were as dramatic as a bombshell. When awakened during bursts of rapid eye movement, subjects had vivid, prodigious dream recall; when no eye movements were present, the subjects rarely remembered anything.

The contrast in recall between the two different times of awakening was about as clear-cut a result as one can ever hope to obtain in science. Now obviously, how we define "dreaming" matters. A fleeting thought may or may not be a dream; but certainly a vivid, complex "real" experience with characters, emotions, maybe a definite plot, qualifies as a distinct dream. Subjects awakened during REM bursts remembered such unambiguous dreams about 80 percent of the time. Another 10 percent of the time, they recalled thoughts or images that could not unambiguously be classified as the absence of dreaming.

These were exciting times. The emerging relationship between REM periods and dream recall was indisputable. Awakened subjects gave long, vivid, complex dream reports time after time, with the additional immediacy of the emotion and excitement of the dream. Equally impressive was the absence of such recall when the awakenings were carried out during the periods when the sleeper's eyes were completely still. As a mere medical student, I was carrying out a host of studies relating the length of the dream to the length of the REM period, and relating the number of eye movements to the amount of activity in the dream— for example, abundant eye movement might be associated with a dream of running around, more restrained eye movement with a dream of just sitting at a table.

At the time, it seemed to me almost as if Aserinsky were embarrassed to be doing research on such a frivolous thing as dreaming, and Kleitman regarded it as just another brick in the house of sleep. I, on the other hand, was overwhelmed with excitement. The fact of the matter was that I was the only one in our trio who took Freud's writing about dreams seriously. Freudian psychoanalysis seemed to permeate every nook and cranny of society in the 1950s, and I was an ardent disciple. I had read and reread *The Interpretation of Dreams* and—along with about half of my medical-school classmates—planned to become a psychiatrist and psychoanalyst. I saw in this physiological marker, REM sleep, the royal road to understanding the dream and, perhaps, the royal road to curing mental illness.

Aserinsky and Kleitman's discovery of rapid eye movements during sleep happened around the same time that Watson and Crick first had their earth-shaking scientific insights about the double helix and ushered in the age of molecular biology. One event launched thousands of scientists on the trail of the genetic code, the molecular expression of heredity, gene therapy, and the fundamental understanding of the genetic regulation of everything. The other discovery had no ready audience except, perhaps, the community of psychoanalysts, who had elevated the dream to a status in psychiatry approximately equal to that of the Pope in Catholicism. Moreover, the discipline of biochemistry was well-established, so it was possible for scientists to exploit the insights flowing from the double helix. The rapid advances often seen in other fields following a major discovery did not occur in our case because there was no "field."

Remember, this was 1952. Although the National Institutes of Health (NIH) existed even in that antediluvian epoch, research grants were very small and relatively rare. The grant that supported our research was about $500 from the Abbott Foundation, and the notion of getting paid to do the research simply did not ever occur to me. In fact, the idea of my becoming a sleep researcher like Kleitman, whose actual professional identity was as a teacher of physiology, was inconceivable. Yet, the chance to satisfy my curiosity about this mysterious phenomenon—dreaming—and its importance to psychoanalysis and mental illness was exciting indeed.

And So I Began My Own Research

In the summer of 1953, Aserinsky got his Ph.D. and left Kleitman's laboratory; at the same time, Kleitman went on sabbatical and buried himself in the scholarly work required for the second edition of *Sleep and Wakefulness*. I was left as the only person in the world, so far as I know, who was staying up all night long to observe sleeping human beings. During my third year in medical school, then, I had the entire Kleitman laboratory all to myself and was left more or less to my own devices.

What, exactly, was my domain? It was a standard two-room laboratory of the times; heavy marble table tops, sinks, Bunsen burner outlets, and metal bookcases. Because we were doing sleep research, one of the rooms became a makeshift bedroom. In the middle of this relatively small "bedroom" was a heavy laboratory table that could not be moved. We had covered the window so that light could not come in; under the fume hood against the opposite wall, we set up a World War II army cot. The brain-wave machine was outside the door, in the "observation" room. A long cable ran from the machine, under the door between the two rooms, to the head of the bed, where we had fastened the box into which we plugged the electrode wires from the subject's head. In those dark ages, there were no transistors; amplification was carried out by means of vacuum tubes. (I wonder what percent of the American population can remember them?) Amplification of bioelectric signals as minute as brain waves was not an easy task. Looking back, it seems as if I spent half of my time fiddling with this apparatus to keep it working.

Despite the freedom I had in Kleitman's lab, my first truly independent research did not take place there. It grew out of my fascination with dreams and their possible correlation to mental illness. Freud never said this in so many words, but several of his followers did—dreams allowed libidinal energy to be discharged. If the energy were not discharged, it would eventually erupt in the waking state as psychosis. This "libidinal safety-valve" theory of dreams really captured my imagination. I scoured the psychiatric literature for studies of dreaming in schizophrenics. There was very little, but one author claimed that schizophrenics did not dream. "Aha!" I said. "We can prove this by studying rapid eye movements in schizophrenics." With this hypothesis and a two-page research proposal, I approached the head of psychiatry at the University of Chicago School of Medicine, Nathaniel Apter, who had a project at a mental institution about forty miles out of the city.

So, as a junior in medical school, I began my research at the state hospital in Manteno, Illinois. This was before the advent of tranquilizers; chronic schizophrenics were still kept in state hospitals, and the wards were crowded with a rich population of actively psychotic individuals. The favored treatments for the various mental disorders were psychosurgery (i.e., lobotomy), insulin shock therapy, psychotherapy, and electroshock therapy.

Using electroencephalography, I studied both schizophrenic volunteers and medical students who were working at the hospital. (When I later reported on my research that the medical students were not significantly different from the schizophrenics, I recall an associate joking that he had known *that* all along.) Many patients would not volunteer—and of course I could not force them— but some did; these I was able to record and awaken during REM periods, just as I had done with subjects in Kleitman's lab. After a few weeks, I realized that my theory—that schizophrenics were crazy because they did not dream—was wrong. In fact, they all had regular periods of REM sleep with voluminous eye movement, and all reported dream content to the best of their ability.

After the fall at Manteno, I was once again working two nights a week in Kleitman's lab as a full-time third-year medical student. In blatant violation of principles I now routinely and loudly proclaim, I became extraordinarily sleep-deprived. If I sat in the back of any classroom, I would fall asleep and snore, thereby attracting the attention of the professor, who would promptly order me out of class. If I sat in the front row to keep myself from falling asleep, it became even more obvious when I inevitably did. I was even summoned once to the office of the Dean of Students to discuss my apparent problem of staying awake in class. Despite the drawbacks, the work was so exciting that I could not stop.

In the early days of all-night sleep research, we felt that using large amounts of oscillograph paper was wasteful, so I would record the brain wave patterns of sleeping subjects for only a minute or so, every ten or fifteen minutes. But gradually I began to record continuously, and when I did, it soon became obvious that sleep was highly organized, with REM periods recurring in roughly ninety-minute cycles, separated by consistently patterned stages of "non-REM" sleep. No one had ever suspected this before. I created definitions for these sleep stages and began to track them in detail through the course of an entire night. I published my results in 1957 in a paper that had taken me about two years to write—as a student, I felt no pressure to publish or perish; and, because I was the only person in the whole world doing this work, there was no sense of urgency to avoid being scooped. Though the paper received little notice initially, it was to become one of the most-cited scientific papers of all time.

By 1957, I had earned my M.D. and a Ph.D. in physiology from the University of Chicago. That summer I left Chicago and moved with my wife to New York City, where I was to intern at Mount Sinai Hospital.

Even though I was excited about our findings based on observations of scores of volunteers sleeping in our laboratory, some skeptics persisted in suggesting that the electrodes we attached near the eyes actually caused or stimulated those movements in some way; if these electrodes were not attached, they speculated, there would be no eye movement. In addition, in those early days, we were not at all sure that every human being would show REM sleep. In order to test these notions, I decided simply to observe large numbers of sleeping people. So, as an intern working nights, I took my personal research to the wards of Mount Sinai Hospital. I would watch a sleeping patient for about five minutes, the limit of my visual concentration. I reasoned that if a patient were in a REM period, I would see a burst of eye movement, and if he or she were not, I would see nothing. If rapid eye movement occupied about 20 percent of the night, as our laboratory studies had indicated, I figured that I should see eye movements in one out of five to ten patients. Occasionally patients would either wake up spontaneously or be awakened by some clumsiness on my part and open their eyes, startled to discover a stranger's face six inches away. A few may have thought they were being visited by the Angel of Death dressed in white.

Suppose We Took Away REM Sleep

While I was at Mount Sinai, in 1959, I began my studies of "dream deprivation." It was actually REM deprivation, but I say dream deprivation because I theorized at the time that dreaming was *always* associated with REM sleep and *only* with REM sleep. Although my earlier studies with schizophrenics had not been very promising, I still had in the back of my mind that dreams were somehow a necessary psychic safety valve, and that if they were prevented, individuals might begin to show symptoms of psychosis.

At the same time, the late Charles Fisher, a Mount Sinai psychiatrist and a disciple of Freud, was studying dreams by talking to volunteers in the daytime. He supported my plan to dream-deprive human volunteers. The procedure was straightforward. We monitored them while they fell asleep and awakened them immediately upon every onset of REM sleep, thus preventing its continuance. In short order, we discovered "REM pressure," a steadily increasing frequency of arousals that are needed to prevent REM sleep from occurring. It was very difficult to maintain total, or near-total, REM deprivation for long periods of time because the number of required awakenings became so large. We also observed the so-called REM-sleep rebound– the increase in REM-sleeptime during the first uninterrupted recovery night.

The psychoanalytical movement was at its zenith at this time. Biological psychiatry–the modeling of mental illness along biochemical and pharmacological rather than psychoanalytical lines– was just beginning. In the next few years our REM-deprivation findings, and confirmation of them, made me a celebrity in psychiatric circles, because I had apparently confirmed the Freudian theory of psychic energy and of dreaming as the safety valve of the mind. We assumed that if we continued the REM-deprivation procedure, the psychic energy would erupt during the waking life as hallucinations and psychosis.

During the 1960s, money for scientific grants loosened up and research boomed. Maybe there would yet be a breakthrough in the search for the purpose of REM sleep. I continued to do REM-deprivation studies after I moved to Stanford in the winter of 1962-63. Some years before, at the University of Chicago, I had collaborated on the earliest studies of REM sleep in cats with Professor Kao Liang

Chow. At the time, he could not believe that the wide-awake brain-wave pattern characteristic of REM sleep was indeed a true sleep pattern—nor could anyone else, for that matter. In the intervening years, Chow had joined the Stanford Department of Neurology, and now we joined forces to begin some REM-deprivation studies in cats. There was no animal laboratory space, but I was temporarily assigned a vacant house at Stanford in which to carry on our studies, with grant money funding a host of Stanford students and employees to help us.

In these studies, a very gentle procedure enabled us to achieve tremendous durations of REM-sleep deprivation, up to seventy consecutive days. No cat ever showed a deleterious effect, but the following changes were noted: The cats grew more active. They became voracious eaters and highly sexed. Their nervous systems became more excitable. The muscle twitches normally associated with REM periods became tremendously accentuated, as did the bursts of eye movements. It thus appeared that the elimination of REM sleep enhanced drive-oriented behavior and, in some way, increased brain excitability.

Sleeping Like a Baby: Forever Dreaming

But the collected REM-deprivation studies were yielding no particular evidence that REM sleep was vitally necessary to the adult organism, so that's what I reported at a scientific meeting in 1965. What, then, could be the function of REM sleep? I fell back on the theory I was developing with Howard Roffwarg, then at Columbia Presbyterian Medical Center, that REM sleep's major role was in the early development of the nervous system. (This, of course, did not rule out the possibility that some abnormality in REM sleep was the basis of psychosis.)

My first scientific observation of infants had been in the nursery of newborns at the University of Chicago hospital in 1955. The question we were exploring at that time was, When does dreaming begin? Kleitman had hypothesized that dreaming would develop as waking consciousness developed, and thus would be absent in neonatal life; so I was watching sleeping newborns, looking for the presence of REM sleep. Within an hour, I had discovered REM in the newborn. Furthermore, I noticed that infants often dropped from clear-cut wakefulness immediately into sleep with rapid eye movements. This was in contrast to what we consistently saw in adults, whose rapid eye movements usually did not begin until about an hour after they fell asleep.

In about 1960, while I was living in New York City, Howard Roffwarg and I undertook the observation of newborn infants at Columbia Presbyterian. We quickly confirmed that, unlike the human adult, newborn infants had a great abundance of REM sleep; furthermore, it was equally abundant around the clock. Since infants were known to sleep some sixteen hours a day, we calculated that the typical newborn infant would spend eight hours every day in REM sleep, and the typical fetus even more. In a newborn kitten, virtually 100 percent of all sleep is REM sleep. Animals that are very mature at birth, in contrast to newborn humans or kittens, tend to have much less REM sleep in their neonatal period.

Our theory, which we published in 1966, is still viable 25 years later–partly because it has a compelling logic and partly because it is extraordinarily difficult to test. According to our theory, intense neural activity is necessary for the proper maturation of the nervous system, and one of the primary (if not *the* primary) purposes of REM sleep would be to provide this activity–as organized patterns of genetically determined behavioral programs–for the developing nervous system. This theory would account for REM sleep being so abundant in the newborn infant. After all, what could newborns be dreaming about all the time, since they have so little waking experience to draw from? It's attractive to think of REM sleep as a time to test the circuits, as it were; to reinforce and carve various synaptic connections while the rest of the system is "down." Then, since much of the nervous system's growth is complete at one year or so, huge amounts of REM sleep are no longer necessary.

But how do you prove this? The obvious way is to prevent the newborn organism from having REM sleep and see what happens to brain maturation. Unfortunately it is almost impossible to prevent the occurrence of REM sleep in a newborn without doing something that itself could be very damaging to the organism. The conventional method of REM deprivation–interrupting REM periods at their onset–is good for only a few hours, after which the REM pressure becomes so great that it cannot be overcome in this manner. Attempts to use REM-suppressive drugs in conjunction with REM deprivation have been partially successful. Roffwarg (now at the University of Texas), the main enunciator of this theory, has returned to the problem a generation later and is slowly producing evidence that even brief periods of REM deprivation in newborn kittens can lead to specific deleterious brain changes.

More Puzzles about REM

In 1975, Gerry Vogel at Emory University conducted carefully controlled studies in hospitalized patients in which he found that selective REM deprivation could alleviate severe chronic depression, apparently causing remissions that were very long-lasting. In this sense, the result was as good or better than the most effective pharmacological treatment. Although this study was reported more than fifteen years ago, it has never been repeated by anyone. It leaves a conundrum: If a natural and important state of being is at least partially eliminated, it cures an illness. The results make some sense in that activation of appetite, sexuality, aggressiveness, and so on is generally the direction in which patients need to be moved. In their illness, they have lost their appetite, their sex drive, and their motivation. If REM deprivation enhances drive-oriented behavior, as earlier studies with cats suggested, it may offer a suitable counterbalance.

Very recently, Vogel carried out another series of experiments in rats, depriving them of REM sleep in infancy through a powerful combination of REM-suppressing drugs and REM-onset arousals. The deprivation lasted about a week. When the animals reached adulthood, Vogel found significant differences between the group of rats who had REM deprivation in infancy and the control group. By a number of measures, the REM-deprived rats suffered from depression (insofar as a rat can be depressed.

What is exciting about Gerry Vogel's experiments is that we are beginning to move away from the very naive and simplistic views we held decades ago. The various states of sleep involve highly complex neural mechanisms and anatomical organization. We should therefore not be surprised at almost any manifestation of REM deprivation. For example, as we will discuss in Chapter 6, the brain in REM sleep creates a complete hallucinatory world. The mechanisms and capacities for doing this, obviously, are part of the brain. We can conceive of many ways in which these processes could become abnormal. Perhaps a substance like LSD triggers the REM-sleep dreaming process during wakefulness in some way that is not quite the same as dreaming; perhaps, too, a deranged, disorganized dream process might flood the mind of an actively psychotic schizophrenic patient.

Since the discovery of REM sleep and the initiation of REM-deprivation studies, the possibility of relating REM sleep to learning and memory has been tested many times. Although there have been some tantalizing findings—suggesting that REM sleep may play a role in memory consolidation, that it may affect subsequent learning, and that it may have some role in assimilating unusual information–none of the results have been solidly conclusive. Another hypothesis that has been investigated is that REM sleep facilitates binocular vision in some way.

The search for the meaning of REM continues. In recent studies, Allan Rechtschaffen and his colleagues at the University of Chicago have totally deprived rats of sleep around the clock. In these studies, the inevitable result is death, usually in about sixteen days. A syndrome has been described in which the rats' temperature-regulating ability changes, they develop peculiar sores on their tails, they become extremely debilitated, and they lose weight even though they eat more (a weight loss that cannot be accounted for in terms of heat loss or increased activity). Rechtschaffen has also pursued selective deprivation of REM sleep only, allowing the rats to get substantial amounts of non-REM sleep; at first these rats become hyperactive, but finally temperature regulation and other functions become severely impaired and the rats eventually die. Death in this case requires more time (about forty days) than in the case of total sleep deprivation. These results suggest that REM sleep is vitally necessary, at least in rats. (However, I understand that Rechtschaffen has done new experiments with a different ambient temperature; in this case, the deprivation does not lead to death. It may be that something like the temperature regulation gone haywire is what kills them, rather than the lack of REM sleep.)

Second Fiddle to a Quark

While much remains to be learned, at this time we know the following about REM sleep. It is a fundamental part of a basic sleep cycle. The rhythmic alternation of REM and non-REM sleep is found in all mammalian species. REM sleep appears to be vitally necessary, although experiments demonstrating this remain controversial. There is strong evidence that REM sleep plays a role in the regulation of mood and/or drive; that it is related in some way to excitability of the central nervous system; and that its suppression may in some way jeopardize the learning and memory functions. The occurrence of large amounts of REM sleep among newborn infants remains possibly the most provocative puzzle of all; it suggests a very important role for REM at the earliest stage of life. When will we learn more?

As I write these words, the United States is in the process of developing a superconducting super-collider in the vicinity of a small Texas town. This super-collider, which will cost billions of dollars, is designed to study the nature of matter and energy at the level of the quark. Meanwhile, only a few pennies of government research money are going to study the specific biological function of REM sleep. What I have learned during my career is that science is becoming ever more political. The reason so much money is being spent to understand quarks and so little to understand REM sleep is simply that the high-energy elementary-particle physicists have directly persuaded Congress to fund their work.

It is my guess that many of our legislators have never heard of REM sleep–or even if they have, certainly don't have a clear idea of what it signifies. Sleep occupies one-third of our lives, and the quality of that third totally determines the quality of the other two-thirds–yet understanding sleep is not a national mandate. Think about it. *We spend a third of our lives sleeping and dreaming and we still do not know why.* It is my highest priority to change the way society deals with sleep—to change public awareness, and to change our national research priorities. Let's not close the book on "The History of REM Sleep." It deserves many more chapters in the years to come.

3

What Is This Thing Called Sleep?

O ur earth and sun spin through the cosmos, with earth turning on its axis every 24 hours. As one side of the planet turns away from the sun and darkens, more than two billion people are going to sleep, or trying to; on the other side, a similar number are ending their sleep and spending their daylight hours awake for the most part. What is this thing called sleep? What is the journey through the night that we must all travel?

It seems a reasonable assumption that the dramatic 24-hour fluctuations of our environment have had a marked influence on human evolution, and that our daily rest/activity cycles represent an evolutionary adjustment. We can ask, therefore, had we evolved on a planet where one side was always in daylight, would sleep as we know it have evolved nonetheless? Must sleep be part of existence no matter what? If some necessary activity of the brain takes place preferentially—or only—during sleep, could this same activity occur in the waking brain if sleep did not exist? And if not, could we exist?

Our two alternating modes of existence, sleep and wakefulness, provide the background for every human function. On a moment-to-moment basis, we may seem relatively flexible in our sleeping and waking behavior; with the help of alarm clocks and invigorating showers, we can wake up and do things at almost any time of the day or night we choose. But the need to sleep has an awesome power over our lives. If we deprive ourselves of it to any significant extent, the drive to sleep quickly becomes more important than life itself. We cannot stay awake even to avoid death. Thus, the train crews that met with a head-on collision near Thompson, Pennsylvania, at 5:30am on January 14, 1988, died because they fell asleep, even though they must have known that falling asleep could spell doom. The overwhelming difficulty of staying awake for more than two or three days, and the willingness to put our lives at risk in order to obtain a little sleep, strongly suggest that sleep is vitally necessary for the health and survival of the organism.

In any case, human beings spend an enormous amount of time sleeping. We organize our work, our recreation, our very society to meet the demands for sleep. Caves, huts, houses, apartment buildings, all clustered together, allow human beings a measure of safety and security, the better to pass the night in the arms of Morpheus.

Early theories about sleep suggested that it was a simple response to the environment; that is, the enfeebled stimulation of darkness was thought to be insufficient to sustain wakefulness. This notion was coupled to the general beliefs that only supernatural beings peopled the dark, and that life as we know it was carried on only in the sunlight. We now know that sleep is not merely a "time out," that life and activity are as much a part of the night as of the day, and that high levels of brain function are as much a part of sleep as of waking life. But we have not yet answered to our satisfaction the question, What *is* sleep?—let alone perfected a means of measuring and studying it.

How Can We Define Sleep?

External appearances aside, the essential difference between normal wakefulness and normal sleep is *the direction of perception*. In wakefulness, we perceive and are conscious of the external world; we are engaged with it, and we respond to it. Wakefulness fosters our ability to find food, to reproduce—in other words, to survive in the real world.

The fundamental essence of sleep, in contrast, is a disengagement from the outer world, accompanied by an engagement with the inner world and the dream world—that peculiar periodic consciousness in sleep. This disengagement from the outer world is an active process in which sensory input is blocked or modified to effect a complete perceptual shutdown; to all intents and purposes, we are blind and deaf. Even if our eyelids are taped open during sleep, we do not see. We know that signals are received by the retina, transmitted to the thalamus and to the visual cortex; likewise, sound is processed by the auditory system. Yet we have no idea why, the second before sleep descends, we see an object in the real world, are conscious of it, perceive it; while the second afterwards, we are subjectively blind and do not see it at all. Nor can we explain why, during REM sleep, stimuli may enter the brain to be "misperceived" in strange and interesting ways.

How the brain alters its state at the moment of sleep onset remains a great mystery, primarily because so little work has been done on the problem. In my undergraduate "Sleep and Dreams" classes, I like to challenge my students to capture the moment of sleep. "Is it cataclysmic?" I ask. "Do your senses seem to explode? Does it seem as if a guillotine falls?" Uniformly, they are unable to report the experience. "I was lying there in bed, waiting for the moment of sleep," they say, "and suddenly it was morning."

Watching subjects in the laboratory, an experimenter cannot fail to be impressed with the abruptness of the moment. One instant, the subject is seeing and hearing and responding to perceptions; the next instant, an iron shroud has fallen over the perceptual apparatus. Of course, the sleeper can be immediately aroused, and if this is done (rarely voluntarily), images can often be recalled; indeed, the mental change associated with sleep appears to be a conversion from abstract thoughts to concrete images. But as to how this is accomplished, there is not really one shred of evidence. The same applies to waking up.

Beyond this disengagement from the outer world, how might we define the sleeping state? In 1913, the French physiologist Henri Pieron proposed the following short definition: "a suspension of sensory/motor activities, characterized by an almost complete absence of movement and an increase in the thresholds of general sensitivity and of reflex irritability." Pieron qualified his definition by the requirement that the suspension of activity be prompted by internal necessity (something inside us that says "now sleep") and not by external conditions (the gathering of darkness). In so doing, he distinguished it from temporary inactivity of plants and animals, at that time thought (erroneously) to result from the cessation of environmental stimuli.

Pieron's view, sophisticated though it may have been for its time, has become outmoded. His notion of sleep as a "suspension" of activity is uncomfortably close to the popular descriptive stereotype of sleep as the product of an idle brain (obviously, a few vegetative functions are maintained), analogous to a car sitting in the garage with the ignition turned off, the motor is silent. The implication here is that the brain must rest. Yet I do not think it self-evident that the brain needs to rest, any more than the heart needs to stop beating for a few hours every night so it, too, can "rest."

The problem of defining sleep was complicated in about 1960 when we first realized that there existed two entirely distinct states of sleep. Although REM sleep was discovered in 1952,this discovery did not immediately alter the fundamental view of sleep as a single state — "not awake." In fact, REM sleep was originally considered simply a "light sleep," consonant with the Freudian notion that the dream occurs to protect sleep and discourage awakening. Even when I began making all-night sleep recordings, the variations in the recordings suggested to me merely a rhythm in the relative depth of sleep rather than the alternation of two biological states.

One reason we were slow to recognize the significance of REM sleep is that to the unaided eye, the brain-wave patterns observed during REM sleep in humans do not differ markedly from those characterizing the first stage of non-REM sleep. When we began to study cats, however, another story emerged. In cats, the REM-sleep brain-wave patterns are indistinguishable from those of the active waking state. In 1959, we began to recognize that there was active muscular inhibition during REM sleep, along with some dramatic electrical activity recorded as spikes, concurrent with the bursts of rapid eye movements. Gradually we began to recognize enough differences that we could no longer view sleep as a single state. The rapid eye movements that we had discovered in Kleitman's laboratory in the 1950s reflected an underlying, fundamental, biological state which, sleep though it surely was, nonetheless differed so markedly from the remainder of sleep that it rated recognition as an entirely unique state of existence. We came to call the two distinct states REM sleep and non-REM sleep.

REM sleep is a state during which the eyes, moving together, dart about under closed eyelids in rapid bursts of activity; physical movement of the major muscle groups is strongly and actively inhibited, though some movement breaks out in restive twitches; and various forms of involuntary or autonomic activity, such as heartbeat and breathing rate, are irregular and often accelerated. EEG measures of central nervous activity strongly suggest that the brain reaches peak activity during REM sleep. Non-REM sleep, on the other hand, yields a totally different brain-wave pattern—synchronized and slow. It is associated with slower and more regular patterns of autonomic function—body temperature drops, heart and respiratory rates slow down. Non-REM also lacks the eye movements and muscle twitches so visible during REM sleep.

Like these "definitions" of REM and non-REM, most definitions of sleep are stated in terms of its concomitants, and, for the most part, these are superficial indeed. Relative immobility, for example, is a "property" of sleep, but is far from an essential one; after all, what about sleepwalking? Some have tried to define the two phases of sleep in terms of more sophisticated concomitants—the firing rates of individual nerve cells, or metabolism in various areas of the brain. Forced by EEG evidence from REM-sleep studies to give up the notion that sleep generally implies lowered brain activity, many theorists of the day nonetheless continue erroneously to attribute this characteristic to non-REM sleep. The slower pattern of brain waves during non-REM sleep is sometimes assumed to reflect slower firing patterns among individual nerve cells. In general, there *is* a small decrease in firing rate in non-REM sleep compared to wakefulness. But in many areas of the brain, there is no change in rate, while in some key areas, nerve-cell activity is brisk. Even among nerve cells whose function slows, the relatively small degree of decrease hardly conforms to a notion of "the brain turned off"; it may be simply the result of reduced movement and, consequently, the reduction in those sensations produced by muscles in motion.

One exceedingly interesting study in 1965 showed that the blood flow in specific areas of cats' brains was generally *increased* during sleep as compared to wakefulness, and much more so during REM sleep. It is therefore possible to conclude only that non-REM sleep is generally as active as wakefulness and that sleep is unrelated to any substantial overall decrease in nerve-cell activity.

Several studies of brain metabolism have turned up regional differences amid a slight overall decrease in metabolism. Even so, measures of cerebral metabolism and nerve-cell firing may not reflect certain crucial changes. For example, sleep could be a time when the nerve cell, temporarily freed from a devotion to message transmission, devotes itself primarily to the synthesis of key biochemical substances or to the adjustment of its intracellular components. Even if there *is* a decrease in nerve-cell firing rates or a decrease in metabolism, that still doesn't mean there isn't *something* going on.

Imagine, if you will, that you were an alien being, trying to learn something about the nature of human life and activity through aerial surveillance of urban streets. By this method, you might well conclude that a city's most productive activity occurred during rush hour, when the streets are crowded with vehicles moving busily back and forth between various structures. At midday, you might assume things to be more "at rest" because you see much less activity on the thoroughfares. What you don't see, of course, is all the activity going on inside the buildings. Similarly, experiments usually show only the action at the junctions of nerve cells, not inside them; even when nothing is going on *between* them, there may well be interesting things happening *within* them.

In order to clarify the nature of sleep, scientists must first reach a consensus on the key processes that differentiate sleep from wakefulness, and then analyze the underlying mechanisms of these differences. What things are actually going on in the brain during sleep as opposed to wakefulness? Are different genes being expressed? Are different peptides being synthesized? Are clusters of nerve cells functioning together in different ways? As we now know, the single nerve cell carries on incredibly complex intrinsic processes, all the way from gene expression to internal transport of nutrients and the assembly and transport of a wide variety of intracellular molecular structures. Perhaps different states of sleep are accompanied by changes in these intrinsic processes. The possibilities are infinite and could occupy an army of sleep researchers. (Keep in mind that there are one hundred *billion* nerve cells in the human brain and each has perhaps 50,000 connections with other cells, the word "infinite" begins to have real meaning.)

There is so much to study. Precisely what physiological processes underlie dreaming? How organized is brain activity during REM sleep? (Probable answer: *very.*) What is the brain doing in non-REM sleep? How many different things? Is it doing several things that are meaningful, or tens of thousands? Is it repairing itself, or "resting," whatever that means? Of the more than 16,000 neuroscientists studying some aspect of the waking brain or the structural brain, surely some reasonable number ought to turn to these questions about the sleeping brain.

It's often easier to say what sleep isn't than what it is. Sleep is clearly unlike many sleeplike states, such as coma, anesthesia, and trance, in that one can be aroused easily or awakened from it. Another interesting state that resembles sleep in many ways, but in other ways not at all, is hibernation, the process by which some species of animals can lower their body temperature to very near freezing in order to conserve calories and survive in low-temperature environments. When the temperature of the brain is close to zero degrees (centigrade), there is no detectable brain-wave activity. Oddly enough, according to a recent finding in Stanford biologist Craig Heller's laboratory, as an animal arouses from hibernation and its body temperature rises, it looks and acts as if it had been sleep deprived.

Here's a question I get asked a lot— Is hypnosis a state of sleep? In this case, an unambiguous answer is possible. The hypnotic trance can exist only during wakefulness. Hypnosis and sleep are entirely incompatible, although the hypnotized subject can simulate being asleep—and, of course, the word *sleep* is often used in inducing the hypnotic trance. I was at a Chicago nightclub with some fellow sleep-watchers some years ago when the entertainer—who was a hypnotist—paraded out on the stage and, in an amazing coincidence, looked directly at me, pointed his finger, and said, in a very imperious voice: "Sleep!" My colleagues rolled on the floor in laughter. I only wish I had had the presence of mind to put my head on the table as if I had instantly responded to his suggestion.

How Can I Tell If You're Asleep Without Waking You Up?

I frequently fly from coast to coast, and when the flight takes place in the daytime, as it usually does, I always have an interest in how many people are sleeping at any given moment. It is my custom to walk up and down the aisles counting those individuals who appear to be asleep and those who obviously are not. The percentage of sleepers varies but is not uncommonly greater than 50 percent, unless a meal is being served or a good movie is being shown. Of course, some of these people may not be asleep when I am counting them. They may have awakened briefly without moving. They may, in fact, be just resting. But if I say around half of them are asleep, I'm probably not far off.

Firsthand observation is perhaps the simplest of many ways to measure sleep. We can simply look at a person and, because of our past experience, judge whether the person is asleep. For most purposes this is more than adequate; rarely do people who are not asleep lie quietly without moving for long periods of time. (The one great exception is people trying to get a suntan. I have never understood how people can just lie endlessly in the sun, doing nothing, not even reading a book. Perhaps there is more sleep going on than we suppose—despite the serious danger of severe sunburn.) Certainly, simple observation is a safe measure in children between the ages of 8 and 12; as I can testify from my studies, a more alert and restless group does not exist. If you ever observe a 10-year-old lying quietly for five minutes with eyes closed, the odds that this child is not sleeping would surely be a million to one.

Nonetheless, such a measure of sleep is not acceptable to scientists because it is not direct; it is an inference that needs to be independently validated. Another approach is asking people to keep a diary specifying several items—the time of going to bed, the time of falling asleep, the time of waking up, the time of getting out of bed for each successive day for any number of days. Assuming this diary is reasonably accurate, we might then be able to say that a given individual sleeps approximately seven hours a night, or approximately eight, as the case may be. The rub comes when scientists want to know *each time* an individual wakens, however briefly, during the night, or what the blood pressure is doing at any given time, or what kind of sleep is occurring at any given moment, or an endless host of other things going on during sleep.

Another problem is the assumption of accuracy in the diary. Subjective reports about sleep can be very misleading. About ten years ago, Mary Carskadon and I did a study of older individuals in which we carefully tabulated all brief arousals from sleep through an entire night. In the face of our objective documentation of scores of these brief awakenings, individuals completely denied them. I have also done studies in which I awakened young adults scores of times a night, and in the morning heard them say, "What a good night's sleep; I didn't wake up once."

Many measurements—blood pressure, for example—are difficult to obtain during sleep without disturbing the subject. In the late 1800s, two intrepid scientists reported that blood pressure was elevated during sleep. I have always doubted that they were measuring the blood pressure of someone who was actually asleep. Frankly, I can barely get a blood-pressure cuff on a waking person in the daylight, let along imagine completing the process by candlelight with a sleeping subject who might not even be lying in a convenient position. You picture it: tiptoeing into a bedroom, wrapping the blood-pressure cuff around the arm of the sleeping subject, inflating the cuff, and actually taking the subject's blood pressure without awakening the subject. Depending upon the person's degree of surprise or fright, the resulting heart rate and blood pressure could mean almost anything.

The problem of observing sleep continuously without running the risk of disturbing the sleeper was not solved until it became possible to reliably measure the electrical activity of the brain. Because brain-wave voltages are relatively tiny, this required the development of amplifiers and systems that could filter out a lot of other electrical disturbance—for example, the 60-cycle electrical field generated by the appliances, instruments, and wiring that are everywhere in a modern building. In addition, there needed to be some way to display the brain-wave patterns. The middle and late 1930s saw the development of the now familiar ink-writing oscillographs in which amplified and filtered brain-wave patterns were captured by pens moving up and down across slowly moving paper. Today, many researchers have given up paper-and-ink oscillographs in favor of computers, which gather data, store it, analyze it, and display it on video monitors or paper printouts in any way the investigator wishes.

In order to identify, classify, and measure sleep, it is necessary to record the electrical activity of three systems: not only the brain, but the eyes and the muscles as well. (We could measure any number of physiological variables, too—heart beat, blood pressure, hormone secretion, body temperature—but these do not define sleep.) In each case, the method is the same. An instrument called the polygraph allows measurements to be made continuously throughout the night. In the sleep laboratory, tiny electrodes are carefully attached to the subject's scalp and face. The wires are brought together into a bundle and anchored to the scalp in a kind of ponytail, then plugged into a panel on the headboard of the bed, connected by cable to the polygraph. Through the night, the electrodes convey signals to the polygraph, which records them as an EEG (the record of brain activity), an EOG (*electrooculogram*, the record of eye movements), and an EMG (*electromyogram*, the record of muscle activity).

All these waves are meaningless scribbles to the uninformed observer, but if they are recorded in a standard and conventional manner, a night's worth of such scribbles can be interpreted accurately by any knowledgeable researcher. Much the same as an experienced surfer watches ocean waves, the sleepwatcher looks for changes in form and frequency of the electrical waves. So characteristic are the waking and sleeping patterns, just a glance at the data from any short epoch allows the observer to instantly know whether the subject is asleep and what kind of sleep it is.

What do the brain-wave patterns of a sleeping subject tell us? In brief, they reveal that a person cycles alternately through non-REM and REM sleep throughout the night. The healthy adult first drops off into the generally quiescent non-REM sleep, which has four successively deeper stages. Non-REM sleep is regularly broken by a period of REM sleep, the characteristics of which are similar to the patterns of alert wakefulness, with the key exception that the body is immobilized.

The figure shows a typical pattern of the alternating stages of sleep through an eight-hour night. Just after sleep onset, a person is in Stage 1 non-REM for only about five minutes. This is essentially a transition period. Thought patterns may continue, but there is a characteristic shift from the abstract to the visual image. Sleep-onset imagery generally does not have the hallucinatory intensity or completeness of REM period dreaming; nonetheless, these transformations are of interest in and of themselves. For example, a writer I know, lying in bed thinking about the impending visit of his mother-in-law and how it would interrupt his work on a current book, suddenly saw an entire bookcase about to topple over on him. He awoke with a start and, being a creative type, instantly grasped the symbolism.

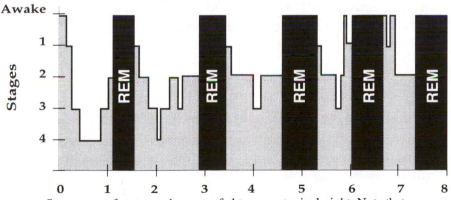

Sequences of states and stages of sleep on a typical night. Note that there are four progressively deeper stages of non-REM sleep.

After sleep onset, a healthy individual progresses rather quickly to Stage 2 sleep—still a fairly light sleep, but with reduced mental activity. After about twenty minutes at Stage 2, the sleeper passes into the deep sleep of Stages 3 and 4. Left undisturbed, the first deep sleep of the night will continue for another thirty to forty-five minutes. Then, about an hour after sleep onset, the sleeper passes briefly through the lighter Stage 2 non-REM and into REM sleep. During the first REM period, which lasts for about ten minutes, dreaming is apparently continuous.

There are usually about five such cycles in an eight-hour period, occurring at roughly ninety-minute intervals. Non-REM sleep grows progressively lighter as the night wears on, while the periods of REM sleep tend to last longer with each successive cycle. Typically twenty minutes long at the end of the second cycle, REM periods of almost an hour's duration are not uncommon toward the end of the night. Most of the deep, Stage 3-4 sleep occurs in the first half of the night. An adult may spend as much as half the night or more in Stage 2 sleep, and another 25 percent of the time in REM sleep.

Sleep Across the Life Span

Each stage of human life tends to have its own characteristic daily sleep/wake pattern. It may even be—who knows?—that the specific role or roles of sleep change as we go from one age to the next, perhaps serving the development of the nervous system in infancy, the healing or maintenance of the nervous system later on. Pathologies of sleep grow more prevalent in later years, but problems occur throughout the life span.

While tots' sleep is typically placid, *studying* their sleep is anything but that. Young children are particularly difficult to research because of their fearfulness. While I was at the University of Chicago, I was once able to coax a 5-year-old who lived next door to me to come into the laboratory with her mother. Though she was obviously tense, not having the faintest idea what was going on, she allowed me to tape electrodes to her scalp and reference electrodes on her earlobes. In this way I got the first all-night EEG sleep recordings of a young child.

The next morning I was able to get the little girl's scalp electrodes off fairly easily with acetone, but the electrodes on her earlobes were another matter. Whenever I gave the adhesive tape a little tug, painfully pulling her hairs, she began to cry. Finally, I simply cut the blue electrode wires, leaving about an inch protruding, and jokingly said, "Well, now you have earrings." She left happily with her mother.

One week later I drove by the apartment house and saw the little girl out playing, the blue wires and electrodes still in place. Either her mother had chickened out, just as I had, or the girl was enjoying a new status with her makeshift bangles and refused to give them up. I like to imagine her now as a mother herself, with teenaged children—and with electrodes still taped to her earlobes.

Infants are actually easier to study than older youngsters not the least because they do so much sleeping around the clock. In the late 1940s, Nathaniel Kleitman wanted to find out how much newborn infants actually sleep. Through painstaking observations by parent volunteers, he established that the total sleep time per 24 hours was about sixteen. We have since found that of these sixteen hours, approximately half consist of REM sleep. Unlike adults, infants usually drop immediately from relaxed wakefulness into REM sleep, without passing through non-REM first. Also, newborns apparently do not experience Stage 4 (very deep) non-REM sleep; this develops during the first year of life.

Although voluntary muscles are totally paralyzed in REM sleep in both adults and newborns, the overall period during which rapid eye movements occur in babies looks very active and restless. REM periods in newborn infants tend to be interrupted every few minutes, usually by a four- to five-second writhing body movement. It is as if the infant wakes up, or at least is partially awake, while this bodily movement is going on. Eyelid closure is often incomplete in newborn infants, and, indeed, when rapid eye movements are vertical, the lids sometimes open. Breathing also is very irregular. In brief, during REM sleep, the infants almost seem to be awake, and for a time, Kleitman maintained that they were. Nonetheless, because I had observed unambiguous rapid eye movement during sleep in older infants, I knew that this newborn writhing was actually indicative of REM sleep.

The newborn infant, then, sleeps about sixteen hours daily, usually in short stretches of two to four hours, with fairly wide individual variations. Sleep time decreases fairly rapidly over the first year as the infant spends more and more time awake in the day—and sometimes in the night, to the great distress of his or her parents. Gradually the developing infant consolidates wakefulness into longer periods, finally interrupted by only one or two naps during the day. By their first birthday, most children are sleeping twelve to fourteen hours a day, most of it through the night.

Regular napping continues until about the age of 2 or 3, again with tremendously large individual differences. These differences are probably also cultural, as some cultures favor napping and other cultures suppress it. Children nearing 10 years of age, whom we have studied fairly intensively in the Stanford Summer Sleep Camp, sleep soundly—and I mean, they are *hard* to wake up—for about 9 1/2 hours. During the day they do not nap and are quite energetic.

During adolescence, as I pointed out in Chapter 1, the need for sleep appears to increase to ten or more hours a night. Unfortunately, in early adulthood, sleep is greatly buffeted by the stresses and distortions of our modern but ignorant society; few high school and college students get the sleep they apparently need. This probably explains why it is virtually impossible to dislodge some teenagers from their beds in the morning.

The need for sleep seems to taper off somewhat with adulthood, although not for everyone. Some individuals continue to need around nine hours, others only eight or less. Individual variability may explain the tremendous differences in sleepiness that we observe among young adults. In general, adults have a decreasing amount of Stage 4 sleep; youngsters may get two or more hours of deep (Stage 4) sleep each night, while adults generally get less than one hour; in old age, Stage 4 sleep may disappear entirely.

Nowadays, we define the need for sleep at any age as the amount required to maintain a reasonable level of alertness in the daytime. Information on sleep requirements for the middle-aged is sparse; only on seniors have data comparable to those on adolescents and infants been gathered. It is commonly thought that the need for sleep declines markedly with advancing years; but this is not the case. Rather, just as in every other system—cardiac, pulmonary, digestive, and so on—old age brings with it a series of age-related changes in sleep patterns. One such change—which, in spite of its striking magnitude, has been overlooked by almost everyone because of the technical difficulty of doing research—is sleep fragmentation.

Indeed, fragmentation is the most predominant feature of older people's sleep. While still directing the Summer Sleep Camp, Mary Carskadon, along with Stanford undergraduate Ed Brown, looked at the number of times older subjects awoke briefly. By "brief," I mean arousals of just a few seconds—so short you don't even know you're awake, yet the change in brain waves clearly marks an interruption of sleep. Ordinarily no one keeps track of awakenings that are very brief—from two to thirty seconds—because ignoring them makes scoring a lot easier and provides a degree of standardization to the scores. This is surely a major error, because when Carskadon and Brown carefully scrutinized the records of 24 healthy, elderly subjects and then did another study with sixteen more, the results were astounding. In the first group, they found an average of 160 of these transient arousals each night, with a range from about fifty to 350; the mean for the second group was 76 brief awakenings. Thus, there was almost no real continuity of sleep, and in a few cases, sleep was interrupted *almost every minute or two!* Carskadon and Brown were able to link these interruptions to a corresponding daytime sleepiness. Little wonder that a common stereotype of advanced age is the image of Grandpa nodding off repeatedly in his rocking chair.

As I write this book, I am 63 years old. Given what I know about sleep in older individuals, I look ahead with some trepidation. However, there is enormous variability, and it is possible that my main sleep predisposition will be largely determined by the genes passed to me from my mother. I do not believe she has ever taken a sleeping pill. At the age of 101, though her mental powers are failing somewhat, she still enjoys good sleep. And at 101, who could ask for more?

4

Making It Through the Night

I just couldn't sleep last night.

—any one of some 80 million Americans
Gallup survey, June 1991

I don't know exactly when it finally dawned on me that I and my fellow sleepwatchers were completely ignoring one of the biggest issues in our territory—insomnia. At least, we certainly weren't giving it the attention it deserved. I guess I had unconsciously bought into what everyone else in the medical profession seemed to believe— that insomnia is a neurotic complaint, generally of no health consequence.

While we are now in a position to alleviate some of the human suffering from insomnia as well as many other sleep related problems, this is a relatively recent development. Early in the game, we sleepwatchers had hitched our wagon to the star of psychoanalysis, Freud, and psychiatry; we expected our findings to have the most relevance to mental, not physical, health. However, as noted earlier, simple links between dreaming and psychosis or other forms of mental illness could not be substantiated, and we were forced to cast around to find the right niche for sleep research.

Not until the 1960s were polygraph recordings widely available to tell us what was happening, physically, in the various bodily systems during sleep. Even then it was another decade, 1970, before patients who specifically complained about sleeping difficulties actually had their sleep examined by doctors with the intent of *treating* the problems.

Given what we know now—that sleep is highly active and organized—it is no surprise that there can be many disruptions and impairments of its functions and mechanisms. When sleep researchers finally began to pay attention to people who complained about their sleep or about their inability to stay awake, they found many hitherto unknown sleep disorders, in surprising abundance.

The "First" Sleep Disorder: Narcolepsy

My entry into what would become the field of sleep disorders medicine was through the door marked *narcolepsy*. In the late 1950s and early 1960s, I accumulated some clinical experience with this fascinating illness, whose manifestations include continual sleepiness unrelieved by sleep; mysterious attacks of sudden muscle weakness or paralysis, termed *cataplexy*; and what we call *hypnagogic hallucinations*—vivid and often frightening images occurring just at the transition from wakefulness to sleep.

When I was in medical school in the early 1950s, narcolepsy rated a single paragraph in my neurology textbook, which described it as a rare variant of epilepsy. As I became more and more committed to the study of sleep, I wanted to observe a narcoleptic patient, but for several years none came my way. Finally, in 1958, my then-colleague at Mt. Sinai Hospital, Charles Fisher, was psychoanalyzing a patient with narcolepsy and suggested to me that this patient should have an all-night sleep recording.

I remember the first night vividly. The recording revealed, in a totally unambiguous manner, something very dramatic that I had seen in infants but never before in an adult—an immediate transition from wakefulness into full-blown REM sleep. Within ten minutes, I knew we had made an important discovery, if it could be generalized.

Fisher and I searched high and low for additional patients with narcolepsy in New York City (population base at the time, 10 million plus) and finally identified four more, all of whom did the same thing—dropped off immediately into REM sleep, instead of sleeping quietly for an hour or so before REM started. I discovered that two colleagues in Chicago, Allan Rechtschaffen and Gerry Vogel, had also stumbled onto this phenomenon, and we pooled our data (nine patients!) for a publication.

When I came to Stanford in January 1963, I was determined to pursue studies of narcolepsy. My interest in REM sleep had given me some ideas about what the narcoleptic abnormalities actually signified. But in my first weeks at Stanford, a concerted search through the records of neurologists and other local physicians failed to identify a single patient who had received this diagnosis.

I have always felt that "one time proves it"—if there was even one, there must be many more. We found five narcoleptic patients in New York; why not here? So I tried something I'd never done before in my life. I put a want ad in the *San Francisco Chronicle*, to this effect: "If you are sleepy all the time and have attacks of muscular weakness when you laugh or get angry, please call Stanford professor." More than 100 people responded; of those, about fifty seemed to have bona fide symptoms of narcolepsy.

Since I did not have a laboratory in my first months at Stanford, I borrowed the clinical EEG laboratory and studied a number of these apparently narcoleptic patients on weekends to see if they had sleep-onset REM periods in the daytime as well as at night. They did; as they were falling asleep, these patients became totally paralyzed and began to show rapid eye movements. Paralysis is, as we know, a normal component of REM sleep. In narcoleptic patients, however, it is pathological—a disturbance in the mechanisms of REM sleep.

By 1964, I had observed almost 100 patients with symptoms of daytime sleepiness, cataplexy, and sleep-onset REM. Because there was not one other physician in the Bay Area who was knowledgeable about narcolepsy, I began to assume the responsibility for their clinical management and treatment. That same year Stephen Mitchell and I, thinking that we might possibly have a money-making operation, started a narcolepsy clinic with the notion that patients would pay a fee and we would take care of them. Unfortunately, narcoleptics have a difficult time holding onto their jobs; the clinic went broke in less than a year. It was, nonetheless, the first true clinical service dealing with a sleep problem. Accordingly, I date the conception of sleep disorders medicine to the opening of the narcolepsy clinic in 1964.

Narcolepsy typically begins in adolescence and may be triggered by the brain changes associated with puberty, which increase the need for sleep in all adolescents. Once established, the illness is present for the life of the patient. It is not fatal and can be treated with stimulants. Today's drug of choice in America remains Ritalin, or methylphenidate, a relatively old non-amphetamine stimulant introduced in the 1950s. Our irrational concern about stimulants, carried over from problems of drug trafficking and drug abuse, has created a barrier to developing any better therapy.

Narcolepsy is not the most prevalent sleep disorder, but it has importance beyond its numbers for several reasons. First and foremost, it tremendously impairs patients' quality of life and ability to carry out daily activities, partly because of their excessive sleepiness and partly because of the paralyzing cataplectic attacks, often brought on by simple laughter or anger. Second, the approximately 250,000 narcoleptics in the United States have been represented by a politically active volunteer organization of some 5,000 members since 1975; therefore, narcolepsy research gets some support from the federal government.

Because narcolepsy involves the fundamental processes of sleep, the money that goes into this research may yield important information about the basic mechanisms of sleep. At Stanford, we have a well-established colony of narcoleptic dogs that is helping us in our active search for the narcolepsy gene. By breeding these dogs, we have been able to shed some light on the hereditary character of narcolepsy. Moreover, by molecular-biological techniques, one of our scientists, Emmanuel Mignot, has found what may be the gene responsible for narcolepsy. As it turns out, this gene already has another quite distinct function; it is one of the immunoglobulin genes. This is interesting, because recent research in humans has turned up another association between narcolepsy, cataplexy, and the immune system. Patients with narcolepsy apparently always have an antigen labeled DQB1-0602 on the outer membranes of their white blood cells. These findings certainly implicate autoimmune processes in the pathogenesis of narcolepsy.

Another feature of this disorder is a tendency toward disturbed sleep at night. Although patients experience excessive daytime sleepiness—at a level comparable to that felt by normal people after several nights' sleep loss—their nocturnal sleep does not resemble that of a sleep-deprived person. In fact, it resembles the slumber of a sleep-satiated person, with most of the time spent in light sleep and very little time spent in the deepest non-REM sleep stages—the opposite of what we usually see following sleep loss.

The Breakthrough into Sleep Disorders Medicine

For centuries, one persistent image of sleep has been that of a healing rest. In the face of ordinary illnesses, most people long assumed that whatever problem existed, it could only improve with sleep. Sleep was not a major concern to doctors. Although we had studied sleep scientifically, the practice of medicine for all intents and purposes ended when the patient fell asleep. In 1970, those of us in sleep research at Stanford decided that if patients complained about their sleep, it was their *sleep* that should be examined, *not* their wakefulness. *This was the conceptual breakthrough* that established sleep disorders medicine.

Taking the logical next step, we opened the world's first comprehensive, fee-for-service Sleep Disorders Clinic and began seeing a patient or two a week. Gradually we developed specialized questionnaires and record-keeping procedures. Within a couple of years, we had developed a clinical practice model in which a physician took responsibility for the patient; when indicated, ordered a diagnostic test that involved an all-night sleep study; and, when a diagnosis was made, also assumed responsibility for treatment.

At the beginning of 1972, we were joined by a French neurologist, Christian Guilleminault, who had been at Stanford for six months in 1970 and had decided to commit himself to sleep disorders. Guilleminault brought knowledge from Europe about a problem called "Pickwickian Syndrome." (The name derives from Charles Dickens's *Pickwick Papers*, in which Joe, the fat boy, is described as falling asleep even when standing up.) In 1965, two groups of European investigators had recorded all-night sleep in such Pickwickian patients and reported periodic *apneas*, or short lapses of breathing during sleep.

In 1969, we had studied two Pickwickian patients at Stanford, and we too observed the periodic lapses in breathing. Attributing it entirely to the patients' marked obesity, we failed to see the significance—that is, we did not recognize that *non*-obese patients with routine complaints of daytime sleepiness or insomnia might be suffering from similar dramatic respiratory problems.

Our understanding changed radically in 1972, when we were testing a thin patient who complained of insomnia. One night we were observing some rather alarming periodic heartbeat irregularities; Guilleminault finally went into the room and discovered that they were connected with episodes wherein the patient was *not breathing*. Indeed, we soon determined that the patient stopped breathing hundreds of times during the night! As a consequence, we immediately added respiratory measures to our routine all-night "polysomnographic" testing. We quickly discovered that many patients who complained of excessive daytime sleepiness actually had breathing problems, which we decided to call *sleep apnea*.

Among the first patients we diagnosed in 1972 were an 11-year-old boy and a 13-year-old girl. Both were overwhelmingly sleepy in the daytime even though they slept through the night. In those days physicians believed, quite erroneously, that excessive sleepiness was caused by depression, low blood sugar, hypothyroidism or other endocrine problems, or encephalitis. These two children had been tested extensively and did not have any of these problems. However, both had high blood pressure, which in the boy's case was progressing to an alarming, uncontrollable, and potentially lethal level. We had become aware that sleep apnea, with its enormous stress on the cardiovascular system, was associated with hypertension and cardiac arrhythmias, but for months we could not convince the other doctors that we knew what was wrong with these children and what to do about it. Like anyone else, academic physicians can be somewhat arrogant and inflexible.

Finally, in desperation—the boy was developing both kidney and heart failure—we were allowed to treat the condition. In 1973, treatment consisted of one thing only: chronic tracheostomy, in which a surgically produced hole in the throat was kept open during sleep, permitting the patient to breathe, and closed in the daytime, when the patient was awake and breathing normally.

The young patient recovered from his surgery with normal blood pressure. The tremendously debilitating, relentless cloud of sleepiness lifted, and an alert young person emerged. Now, pediatricians were more willing to treat the young girl with chronic tracheostomy. In her case, too, all symptoms were almost instantly reversed. Unfortunately, the years of nocturnal oxygen deprivation had produced diffuse brain damage; her measured IQ was now 75, even though she had been of normal intelligence as a small child.

Although sleep disorders medicine had made tremendous advances in just a few short years, one dramatic moment in 1973 really brought home for me the magnitude of what we were dealing with. On this particular night I was standing in the control room, watching the paper emerging from the polysomnograph, when I noticed the subject's heartbeat recording had suddenly gone flat. Thinking this was probably an apparatus failure, I fiddled with the dials, but within four or five seconds I realized that it wasn't the machine. I will never forget the rush of alarm and adrenaline of that moment. Just as I was approaching total panic, the heartbeat resumed. The pause had lasted more than fifteen seconds, corresponding with a long episode of apnea in this patient. Even knowing as much as we did, up to that point we had not fully accepted that our patients were under great risk. The very next day, we instituted a number of procedures at the clinic that would allow us to cope with any emergency.

As the word of our clinical successes spread, excessively sleepy patients began coming to us from all over America for diagnosis and treatment. In 1974, Elliot Weitzman, who had been in my class at medical school, decided to spend a sabbatical at Stanford University. He worked in our clinic for a while and, extremely impressed, went on to develop the world's second sleep clinic—the Sleep-Wake Disorders Center—at his home institution, Montefiore Medical Center in the Bronx. By 1975, five institutions in the United States provided the service of examining patients during sleep—besides Stanford and Montefiore, there were sleep disorders clinics in Cincinnati, Houston, and Pittsburgh.

Up to that point, although patients did sometimes pay cash for our services, their medical insurance companies routinely denied reimbursement because our services were deemed "experimental." We were able to bootleg our clinic losses on research grants because we were, in fact, making discoveries almost daily. Then in 1975 we finally convinced Blue Shield that our services were no longer experimental, and the clinic became self-sustaining. Sleep disorders medicine had truly "arrived."

What Every Person Should Know About Sleep Disorders

Though there are more than a hundred officially recognized diagnoses of different sleep disorders, for the lay person the subject need not be very complicated. All readers of this book ought to finish it secure in their ability to recognize the most dangerous sleep disorders. Careful observation of the sleeper by a spouse or bed partner in all likelihood can create a high level of suspicion and motivate the patient to seek medical help.

There are four broad categories of symptoms that may indicate a sleep disorder, possibly serious: (1) the perception and/or experience of disturbed sleep (insomnia); (2) daytime drowsiness, which may or may not be perceived as due to disturbed sleep; (3) a variety of "abnormal" behaviors occurring during sleep or associated with an apparent arousal from sleep; and (4) loud snoring. One or all of these may be present at the same time.

If you notice such a symptom and wonder if you should be worried, the key issues are duration and severity. Transient sleep problems arise from stress and anxiety, or from temporary problems with a brain mechanism called the biological clock (see Chapter 5). Although a sleep disturbance or daytime sleepiness may be very troublesome, it probably does not indicate a serious disorder unless it has persisted several weeks. While not what we call a *disorder*, transient sleep problems can nonetheless be very dangerous—even fatal—as they may result in a sleepiness-related error or accident like those described in Chapter 1. Such transient sleep problems are usually treated symptomatically. Troubled sleep and daytime drowsiness associated with various medical illnesses and medications are also common.

Obstructive Sleep Apnea

The word *apnea* refers to the absence of breathing. Sleep apnea syndrome is the most important of all the sleep disorders because of its very high prevalence and its threat to life, health, and waking function. This disorder usually appears in the third or fourth decade, mostly in males. The problem can occur (though more rarely) in children and in women, with an increasing prevalence in post-menopausal women. The first sign, typically, is loud snoring, which progresses to snoring with intermittent choking silences. Heavy snoring indicates resistance to air flow in and out of the lungs, and the silences, of course, indicate apnea.

One is predisposed to this illness by a variety of factors that reduce the size of the upper airway: among others, obesity, small jaw, large tonsils, and deviated nasal septum. Sleep itself tends to reduce the tone of upper airway muscles, as well as to impair the highly complex and delicate coordination required for all the muscles of the tongue and throat to open our airway when we inhale. The sleep apnea condition ranges in severity from a few respiratory pauses per night to hundreds. Over twenty respiratory blockages per hour is unambiguously clinically significant; over forty to fifty is severe.

If someone you know is unusually tired, falls asleep inappropriately on occasion, and snores in an annoying manner, the odds are great that the problem is sleep apnea—especially if there is not a clear history of voluntary, chronic sleep deprivation, either because of a personal sleep schedule or an unconventional shiftwork schedule. In particular, any adult male who is overweight, snores loudly, and has a noteworthy tendency to fall asleep in committee meetings, in movies, or after lunch is almost certain to have this serious illness.

The National Commission on Sleep Disorders Research has heard testimony of witness after witness after witness with flagrant and obvious sleep apnea syndrome—falling asleep everywhere and keeping the neighborhood awake with their loud, cacophonous, gasping snoring—who have nevertheless gone ten or more years without being diagnosed. Given the small number of sleep centers in the United States and the number of treatment devices that have been sold, we estimate that about 90 to 95 percent of all sleep apnea victims are, as yet, unidentified. Not only are they a danger to themselves and others on the road, they are also at risk for the development of stroke and cardiovascular disease.

The high incidence of cardiovascular disease in males is due not only to cholesterol, obesity, and genetic factors, but also to obstructive sleep apnea. Periodic apneas are associated with a fall in blood oxygen and a great strain on the cardiovascular system. In severe sleep apnea, life-threatening irregularities or pauses in heartbeat are often seen, as well as very high spikes in blood pressure at night and general hypertension in the daytime.

Sleep apnea syndrome is sufficiently common and sufficiently dangerous that everyone should be aware of it. Although a large scale epidemiological study to establish the general prevalence of sleep apnea in the general population remains for the future, an estimate of between 1 and 4 percent — or 2 to 8 percent of the male population — is probably accurate. The problem increases with age, so that in middle-aged males, one in ten would not be an outrageous number. Stanford students, themselves at very low risk, have told me of innumerable instances in which they have diagnosed one of their parents, often resulting in the parent getting proper treatment— with very beneficial effects. Many sleep apnea patients who have received treatment in our clinic to end their choking and dozing have become activists and have, on their own, identified as many as 25 or more other victims.

Several studies show that 10 to 30 percent of all individuals over 65 have sleep apnea. It is therefore important that *everyone* have some sort of sleep and breathing evaluation in later life. In the San Diego area, a random sampling of the population over age 65 indicated that 25 percent of them suffered from sleep apnea. Many of these cases were mild, but a substantial number were severe.

Still other surveys show that about 10 percent of the general public complain of troublesome sleepiness in the daytime, and most of these individuals also snore. Studies of hospital populations have also been done, along with studies of snoring (which is a symptom of sleep apnea, although not everyone who snores has the illness).

Two new treatments for apnea have virtually completely replaced chronic tracheostomy. One, a surgical procedure, works only in a limited number of patients. In the second treatment, a stream of air is blown gently into the nose all night long, so that the airway does not collapse with inspiration. This treatment is marvelously effective and entails only the inconvenience of carrying a blower everywhere one stays overnight and having a mask over the nose all night long. However, because about 20 percent of patients are unable to comply with this treatment, we are searching for a sleep apnea pill.

Sudden Infant Death Syndrome (SIDS)

The foregoing material should suggest immediately that sleep apnea might be a cause of sudden infant death syndrome or SIDS, the poignant and tragic illness that each year in the U.S. takes more than 7,000 infants from the bosom of their family. The small amount of research on this problem to date has not identified a clear-cut cause; there may be multiple types of events during sleep that lead to death. What is absolutely certain is that SIDS is a sleep disorder and occurs because of some problem the sleeping brain has in maintaining breathing, heartbeat, blood pressure, or some other vital function.

In contrast to the adult sleep apnea patient, who has symptoms and thus gets examined, the infant is dead before anyone knows there is a problem. As Chairman of the National Commission on Sleep Disorders Research in 1990-1992, I have heard testimony from a large number of mothers and fathers of SIDS victims, and I can never hold back my public tears as I try to imagine being one of them. It is just too painful to hear yet another story of a mother who was happily rearing her baby, only to find it suddenly dead in its crib—a woman who can do nothing more for her beloved infant than hold it dead in her arms a moment longer. The means currently exist to monitor large samples of infants to find something that will predict and thereby allow us to prevent such catastrophes. However, thousands of infants would have to be monitored to find the ones at risk for SIDS. But quite frankly, I would rather we spend our tax money doing this than searching for the sixth quark, or building weapons, or sending a few people into orbit around the earth.

PLMS—Another Troublesome Disorder

Another specific sleep disorder, one that is even more commonplace than sleep apnea, is periodic limb movement during sleep, or PLMS. This syndrome was described many years ago in Italy by Elio Lugaresi, who identified it as a neurological problem. That PLMS was a major, common sleep disorder was not recognized until the 1970s, when Christian Guilleminault and I were making all-night observations of patients suffering from insomnia and daytime sleepiness. We reported in 1973 that many patients who complained of insomnia had repeated movements of one or both legs while they slept. This finding convinced us that the polysomnographic exam should always include the recording of muscle activity from the legs. We now know that the prevalence of PLMS increases with age, to about 40 percent of all individuals over the age of 65.

In the typical PLMS patient, involuntary leg movements occur every thirty seconds, plus or minus a few seconds, throughout either the whole night or portions of it. This often vigorous movement can generate hundreds of brief awakenings and create complaints of severe insomnia or of marked daytime sleepiness—often by both patients and their bed partners. Try to imagine your bed partner flexing and thrusting his or her legs like clockwork every 25 seconds for an entire night. After a while, it would be like Chinese water torture.

PLMS does not have the same life-threatening overtones of sleep apnea, but it can be exceedingly troublesome, and in a few patients it appears to progress to a severe "restless leg" syndrome that can be debilitating. People with restless leg syndrome cannot sit still or lie down, because when they do, very unpleasant and distracting sensations begin in their legs, forcing them to get up and walk around until these sensations disappear. Although fairly rare, all patients with restless-leg syndrome have periodic limb movements. For this reason, we speculate that the latter may be a long-term outcome of the former. Researchers continue to search for the cause and for a cure and a better treatment, which today consists of a moderately effective medication.

What We Know about Insomnia

One of the most common complaints of people everywhere is what they usually call insomnia. This rarely means no sleep at all, but rather a troubling or unpleasant number of awakenings during the night, long periods of no sleep, inability to fall asleep, or waking up too soon.

At least one barrier to the diagnosis and treatment of insomnia is the widespread perception that it is a trivial problem, not worthy of a doctor's attention. This issue is finally being put to rest. A comprehensive national survey carried out for the National Sleep Foundation by the Gallup Poll Organization showed that one-third of the general population, approximately 80 million people, suffer from insomnia. Of these, at least one-fourth (or 9 percent of the general population) complained of severe chronic insomnia. In the others, severe bouts of insomnia punctuated their otherwise apparently normal sleep. Much more striking, however, was the evidence of morbidity and, possibly, mortality. The complaint of insomnia, according to the Gallup Poll, is significantly associated with difficulty concentrating, irritability and other emotional problems, a higher rate of automobile accidents, difficulty functioning on the job, and impairment of interpersonal relationships. And, considering all the people who fall asleep behind the wheel of a car, surely there are cases of death as a result of insomnia.

The National Commission on Sleep Disorders Research recently sponsored a nationwide study of primary care clinical practices. The results indicated that knowledge about sleep disorders, including sleep apnea, had barely permeated this level of practice; but even more impressive was the revelation that the specific problem "insomnia" appeared to be nonexistent, if patients' records were to be believed. Among 10 million cases compiled from computerized databases in clinics all over America, not one single specific diagnosis of insomnia was found. Among the carefully scrutinized records of 10,000 patients in primary care clinics, only 73 instances of an insomnia complaint were seen. In no case did the physician's notes indicate an understanding of the problem.

The foregoing should not be perceived as an indictment of physicians. In the first place, surprisingly, the Gallup Poll referred to above showed that most patients with insomnia do not consult a physician, presumably because they share the physician's belief that it is not a clinical or dangerous problem. In addition, and more important, most physicians do not receive one minute of valid educational facts about insomnia in their training. Hence, when a patient does happen to complain of it, they have no idea what to do. When they do suggest something, it is usually out of ignorance and temerity.

One common category of persistent insomnia, called *psychophysiological insomnia,* can be very severe. Typically the patient sleeps better when traveling or on a vacation. The source of the problem is thought to be tension or anxiety about falling asleep. As the patient focuses more and more on this, the bedtime rituals and environment trigger enormous tension. Merely getting into bed is enough to cause hyperarousal. Once identified, this disorder may be treated by counter-conditioning, relaxation therapy, and regaining personal control of the sleep environment. It usually requires several visits to a qualified sleep therapist.

Disorders Rare and Strange

Quite a number of the officially identified sleep disorders seem to be rare, although, I must add that every sleep disorder we have discovered was thought to be rare in the beginning. As awareness increases, its prevalence is typically revised upward.

One relatively rare condition is called *REM sleep behavior disorder* —interesting because, in a sense, it is exactly the opposite of narcolepsy. In this illness, muscle paralysis, which protects the dreamer and is overactive in narcolepsy, fails. Thus when patients dream, they also act. The behavior of victims during sleep is spectacular, often with highly refined speech and total body movement. This is extremely disruptive to sleep and, if frequent, tends to preclude normal amounts of REM sleep. Because the varieties of dream activity are so wide, the illness poses a danger to a bed partner, for example, if the patient should dream of punching someone.

REM sleep behavior disorder is more common in older populations, and may be the result of lesions in the region of the brain that mediates muscle paralysis during REM sleep. This disorder is not the simple sleepwalking and sleep-talking behavior that occurs transiently, especially among children; here, the behavior is sometimes quite complex and violent, and is associated with the experience of dreaming (the correlated dream can often be recalled).

In addition to the foregoing, we see a host of problems that generally involve movement during sleep. They range from very common and benign problems, such as sleep walking, sleep talking, and enuresis, to more disturbing and peculiar disorders. At the most severe, they include night terrors and sleep-related episodes of violence, collectively termed *parasomnias*. Occasionally, these episodes, which represent a breakdown in the brain's suppression of body movement and emotional visceral functions, can be catastrophic for a family. We saw a patient at the Stanford Sleep Clinic who had been arrested for the attempted murder of his father-in-law. What had actually happened is that, while he was still asleep, the patient had assaulted his wife and was trying to choke her; he then attacked and injured his father-in-law, who was attempting to intervene. Had we not been able to establish that this was a sleep disorder and initiate treatment, the patient would have been imprisoned.

A more serious but fortunately exceedingly rare disorder is called *fatal familial insomnia*. European sleep specialists have described two families with this apparently genetically transmitted condition in which the patient eventually dies. (No cases have been reported in the United States, to my knowledge.) The disease begins insidiously, typically in mid-life, and progresses to complete inability to sleep. At about this time other symptoms, including dreamlike waking hallucinations, start to appear. Death usually comes in about a year. At autopsy, lesions are seen in the brain in circumscribed areas of a structure called the thalamus. Some investigators have speculated that it is not these tiny lesions but the insomnia that kills the patient, although this is far from certain.

Common Sense About Sleeping Pills

How is the primary-care physician to diagnose and treat sleep disorders? Until very recently, clear guidelines have been lacking. However we address the problem, though, we quickly come to the controversial issue of sleeping pills.

I should say at the outset that I am presently involved in sleeping-pill research and have been for years. If the federal government has been fainthearted in its financial support of sleep research, the pharmaceutical companies have not. No matter how high-minded or ethical the pharmaceutical industry might be, self-interest always leads to bias. Yet, in all the history of sleeping-pill research, not one sleep laboratory was funded by the federal government's National Institutes of Health until just the past couple of years, when one grant was awarded. This has meant that a truly neutral presence has never existed.

Nonetheless, drug research has made significant contributions to our knowledge base. A study we were doing in 1970-71, to see if daily oral ingestion of 5-hydroxytryptophan would ameliorate the daytime sleepiness of narcoleptics, was directly connected with the development of the Stanford Sleepiness Scale, which offered the world's first measure of this quality or dimension of human performance and function. In 1973, I was asked by the Sandoz Company to study their compound temazepam, or Restoril; the next summer, I undertook a long-term study of another benzodiazepine, Dalmane. These two sleeping-pill studies were our first summer use of Lambda Nu house that became the famous Stanford Summer Sleep Camp, a cornerstone of our sleep research at Stanford for ten years. Using pharmaceutical companies' funds to study the effect of sleeping pills on sleep stages and total sleep enabled researchers to gather baseline data from large numbers of individuals than would have been possible using federal grants alone.

If there is any area of clinical practice where myth and fantasy rather than data dictate what is done, it is in the use of sleep-inducing medications as a symptomatic treatment for insomnia. While the lay press and the pontifical writings of specialists harangue about the dangers of addiction and other side effects, the millions of people who occasionally use sleeping pills say something totally different. In Gallup Poll surveys (designed by Mitchell Balter and his colleagues of the Public Health Research Center in Washington, D.C.) they say that these medications truly relieve their symptoms. They say that they tend to use them infrequently. They say that, should the insomnia problem recur, they would like to use them again. Conclusion: What doctors currently appear to believe and what is actually true are bizarrely contradictory. It is my medical opinion that sleeping pills give excellent relief, are typically needed for only a few nights, and should not be irrationally withheld by the physician.

In recent years, there has been a great deal of negative publicity about benzodiazepines. Medical professionals, like everyone else, watch television programs such as "20/ 20" (and with regard to sleep disorders, this may be their main educational input). In addition, they hear continual uninformed criticisms that physicians overuse sleeping pills. The opposite is actually true. Three entirely independent scientist-directed national surveys by the Gallup Poll have shown that only about 10 percent of patients with serious insomnia complaints receive a prescription for sleeping pills, and even in those cases, they almost never use them for more than a few nights (usually five or less).

Of course, there have been notable exceptions, and some disturbing results with uninformed, unsupervised use. One of my first patients at the Stanford Sleep Disorders Clinic had a pernicious insomnia. As I took her history, I was astounded at her consumption of sleeping pills. Every night at bedtime, she would ingest an amazing total of 8,000 mg of Seconal, phenobarbital, Miltown (meprobamate), and Benadryl, just as she might eat a bowl of Wheaties. This woman would then fall almost immediately into a kind of coma from which she would emerge four hours later, unable to sleep any longer.

I knew that if I suddenly withdrew this amount of barbiturates and other sedatives, she would almost certainly develop seizures and possibly die. A colleague suggested slow withdrawal. I gave the patient permission to call me at any time of the day or night, seven days a week, and I began to reduce her intake of medication by about one clinical dose (for example, 100mg of Seconal) per week. It took more than a year to accomplish the withdrawal, but at the end of that time, she went to bed with no medication whatsoever and slept 6 1/2 hours—*more* than she had been sleeping with enough medication to kill a horse. By then a benzodiazepine tranquilizer called flurazepam (trade name Dalmane) had been developed, and barbiturates virtually disappeared from use.

It was, interestingly enough, a sleeping pill that greatly increased the sensitivity of the Food and Drug Administration to the hidden pitfalls of medication. Thalidomide was a sleeping pill widely prescribed in Europe in the late 1950s and early 1960s and occasionally taken by Americans who were traveling there. As is now well-known, this compound turned out to have severe teratogenic (birth defect producing) potential among pregnant women. Fortunately never approved in the United States, Thalidomide was quickly withdrawn in Europe; but the tragedy of babies born without limbs was only partially averted. The fact is, there is no way to say that any drug is completely safe when used during pregnancy. All drugs, including cigarettes and alcohol, should be eschewed during this period.

Although I would generally classify them as "safe," sleeping pills are not candy. They are therapeutic compounds—much like digitalis, cortisone, or antibiotics—to be used for a specific purpose with care and understanding by a physician who is licensed to prescribe them. If they were totally safe, they would be sold over the counter. However, I have not seen a truly addicted patient for almost twenty years. Excluding a physician who was taking 120mg of Dalmane every night on his own and was falling asleep in the daytime—and eventually had an auto accident—I have never encountered a dramatic adverse reaction. My only real concern with sleeping pills is daytime carryover sedation. Some sleeping pills, notably flurazepam, have a long duration of action, which often causes a troublesome degree of sedation in the daytime. Others, such as triazolam (trade name Halcion), do not generally carry over into the daytime.

Of the currently marketed sleeping pills, I prefer triazolam because it goes to work rapidly and, more important, rarely if ever shows a daytime carryover. My typical approach is to prescribe 0.25mg at bedtime for from one or two nights up to a maximum of three weeks. I *always* ask the patient to call in to report whether relief has been obtained, because I have encountered completely unexpected, idiosyncratic responses to almost every medication I prescribe. When I do not know a patient, I usually prescribe only ten tablets. If a patient I know well wants a supply of medication to use intermittently for travel or transient episodes of stress, and I am quite certain that this patient will follow my instructions to use the medication for only several nights, I do not hesitate to prescribe more—thirty tablets, sometimes as many as fifty. I never give refills. If there is a healthy doctor/patient relationship, there is no danger whatsoever of addiction.

No drug is absolutely, completely, 100 percent safe. Benzodiazepines are safer than many over-the-counter drugs—in particular, aspirin, which in large doses can cause gastric bleeding. When properly used—at the minimum effective dose at bedtime, for short periods, to alleviate transient insomnia—the risk-benefit ratio is extremely positive for both patients and society. This has recently been shown by Mitchell Balter, who compared large numbers of treated and untreated insomniacs and found that the latter had not only far more severe symptoms, but more auto accidents than either treated insomniacs or the general population. Lack of sleep gives rise to dangerous daytime impairment.

A patient with severe, acute insomnia can be compared to a patient who has been severely burned; weeks and months of analgesia are not indicated, but we cannot withhold pain-killers in the face of initial severe pain for fear that the burn patient will become addicted to them. In a sense, withholding the medication that will alleviate an insomniac's suffering violates the Hippocratic Oath.

The Future of Sleep Disorders Research

For years, I have been concerned about the small amount of sleep research that is supported by the National Institutes of Health, particularly research on the fundamental problems of sleep, which is almost nonexistent. I have worked for a number of years in the political arena, both as president of the American Sleep Disorders Association and as a private citizen, in an effort to remedy this enormous gap. In 1988, primarily as a result of our efforts, the Congress of the United States passed legislation creating the National Commission on Sleep Disorders Research, which I have already mentioned several times. Although President Ronald Reagan signed the bill into law on November 4, 1988, it was not until March 1990 that the commissioners (of which I was one) were appointed. This eloquently illustrates the snail's pace of the government bureaucracy.

The commissioners were a highly diverse group, and when I have asked various bureaucrats how they were selected—or, for that matter, how commissioners of anything are selected—I have been told there are two things I should never know: how sausage is made, and how commissioners are chosen. At any rate, our life was set at eighteen months, and as I write, that period is coming to an end.

We have made the following recommendations:

- A massive educational campaign directed at the entire American public, federal agencies, and health professionals.
- A visible entity in the federal government that is accountable for sleep disorders and sleep research.
- A large escalation in training of sleep disorders specialists and researchers.
- Selective but substantial upgrading of research programs, not only in the areas currently being studied—such as the function of sleep, the basic sleep mechanisms, and the pharmacology of sleep—but also in all those areas I have noted where we know almost nothing and there has heretofore been no research.

We are in the process of organizing a grass-roots advocacy campaign, building the constituency of patients and professionals that will help implement our recommendations. We hope for a substantial increase in awareness, to the end that all Americans will realize that sleepiness can kill; that all Americans will know the signs and symptoms of serious sleep disorders; that if they go to their doctor, the doctor will know what to do; that the cost burden of sleep-related accidents will be reduced—and, finally, we hope all Americans will benefit from the increased daytime alertness and energy that comes from adequate sleep at night.

5

The Circadian Rhythm of Sleep

(Or, How I Helped Win the Coca-Cola Bowl, I Think)

L ucky, lucky, lucky me,
  I'm a lucky son of a gun.
I work eight hours and sleep eight hours;
That leaves eight hours for fun!

—Radio jingle from the 1950s

Most of us, like the happy-go-lucky fellow in this jingle, like to think of sleep as a natural behavior that recurs in an orderly fashion every 24 hours, rescuing us from our blessed weariness from work and play. Recently we have discovered a great deal about a powerful determinant of the orderly recurrence of sleep—a determinant, moreover, that is quite independent of the tiring effects of work and play. This amazing device, which we call the biological clock, is housed in two tiny areas of the brain called the *suprachiasmatic nuclei.* The entire mechanism— whether in the brain of a mouse or a human—is about the size of a pinhead, yet its 10,000 component nerve cells each control about 10 million other nerve cells—and thus, indirectly, billions or trillions of cells throughout the body— making it the most powerful control system in the known universe. Its precision is amazing; it has been shown that the biological clock is accurate to within a minute or two each day. Quite possibly in the absence of disturbance over long periods of time, it is even more accurate.

The fact that we know the anatomical location of the clock, and, therefore, can study it directly—its constituent cells, their connections and subcellular structure—using all the powerful techniques of molecular neurobiology, has made research on this tiny nucleus and how it controls behavior perhaps the hottest field of all the neurosciences. This area may soon yield more breakthroughs in our understanding of human behavior; a number of neuroscientists have now entered the race. Because the field is moving so fast—we hear of new experimental results that alter our thinking, literally, on a weekly basis—it is impossible to present a truly up-to-date account here. Therefore, we'll stick with the basics.

The biological clock is the internal timer that governs the repetitive rhythms of the body's systems, such as temperature, hormone secretion, or rate of metabolism. Two properties necessarily describe a rhythm. The first is *amplitude,* or magnitude of fluctuation within one complete cycle. The amplitude of the daily body-temperature rhythm, for example, might be two degrees Fahrenheit. The second important property of a rhythm is its period, or the time it takes for one complete cycle. The period of the daily body-temperature rhythm is about 24 hours. Any biological rhythm with a period close to 24 hours is termed *circadian*. The human body temperature, then, has a circadian rhythm, as does the sleep/wake cycle.

For years no one ever dreamed that there might be an internal clock in control of our bodies, and as recently as 1939, there was no consensus whatsoever that a biological clock existed. Before the invention of the electric light ushered in the 24-hour society, the recurring pattern of sleep at night and wakefulness in the daytime was attributed to the different levels of external stimulation; the bombardment of the brain by light, sound, higher temperature, and movement was thought to keep it awake, while reduction of all these stimuli at night allowed the brain to go to sleep.

In 1939 Nathaniel Kleitman described a transatlantic voyage during which he observed that the passengers sailing eastward tended to sleep increasingly later and miss breakfast, while, sailing westward on the return voyage, they tended to go to bed increasingly earlier, occasionally missing dinner, but never breakfast. Although in retrospect this "boat lag" was clear evidence of the biological clock at work, Kleitman assumed that it merely showed the persistence of a daily 24 hour rhythm that had become conditioned by years of repetition.

Travel by passenger jet has made millions aware of an analogous effect: jet lag. After a flight through several time zones, travelers experience disruption of their sleep/wake cycles as their body time (biological clock time) diverges from local time. Someone accustomed to going to bed at midnight and waking up at 7am in California who then flies to New York will not fall asleep until 3am (New York time) and will want to sleep until 10am.

If you have no problem sleeping through the night or staying awake in the daytime, you know that your biological clock is synchronized to local time. The morning wake-up signal's occurrence—the moment when you feel ready to get up—is a good indicator of your body time or "phase." Another phase indicator is the time of day, typically the afternoon, when midday sleepiness occurs. In individuals whose circadian rhythms are well synchronized, drowsiness tends to occur between 2 and 4pm. If you feel it later, your clock may be phase-delayed; if earlier, your clock may be phase-advanced.

Trying to Study the Biological Clock

Just as the genetic control of inherited traits was discovered by Mendel in the 1800s and then ignored for half a century, the biological clock was actually discovered more than two-and-a-half centuries ago. In a book that appeared in 1729, French scientist Jean Jacques d'Ortous de Mairan wrote about his detailed observation of an internal clock in the heliotrope, a type of plant that opens its leaves daily in the sunshine and closes them at nightfall. After isolating the plant in total darkness, de Mairan found that its leaves continued to open during the regular hours of daylight, even though the plant itself remained in complete darkness. Something internal was clearly keeping time.

More than 250 years later, the fundamental strategy for studying the internal clock remains the same. Isolate an organism from the environmental time cues, particularly those associated with the earth turning on its axis, and see if measurable 24-hour (or near 24-hour) rhythms persist.

In the early days, there was much controversy about whether or not organisms could be truly isolated from electromagnetic radiation, subtle noises, and so forth. Additionally, the isolation from external cues would have to continue long enough to dispel the possibility that any observed pattern was just a persistent learned or conditioned rhythm, as Kleitman had originally conjectured.

Kleitman almost discovered the biological clock in humans in the late 1930s. Seeking to learn more about the sleep/wake cycle, he and a colleague spent thirty days underground in Mammoth Caves, Kentucky, isolated from all grosser environmental fluctuations. Their goal was to discover if human beings could sleep and wake on schedules not based on the 24-hour day. As the two experimenters adopted first a 21-hour and then a 28-hour schedule, Kleitman regularly measured their body temperatures and kept a detailed sleep diary. His companion's temperature and performance partially adapted to the 21- and 28-hour days, but his own failed to do so at all. This stubborn refusal of Kleitman's body to adapt to days of different lengths was a strong clue that the body's daily fluctuations were not mere passive responses to changes in the environment.

By the 1970s, the significance of circadian rhythms and the existence of a biological clock were becoming clearer. It was now known that human beings, living in an underground bunker isolated from all environmental changes and time cues, revert to an endogenous or "free-running" rhythm with a period of about 25 hours. Clearly, like de Marain's heliotrope, people's bodies had a timer that was not dependent on external stimuli.

Over the years, circadian rhythms have been extensively studies in rodents and insects. Even the sea slug and yeast mold have robust circadian rhythms, as do plants and single-celled organisms. Period lengths vary among species. The free-running rhythm in mice, for example, tends to be less than 24 hours, though rarely less than 23; the free-running rhythm in humans tends to be longer than 24 hours. There are also individual differences within species, but even so, the deviation from 24 hours is rarely more than sixty minutes.

How are our circadian rhythms—which, left to themselves, might diverge toward their separate free-running intervals— synchronized, or *entrained*, so that they all recur exactly every 24 hours? Apparently the biological clock can adjust its phase in response to certain external time signals. In normal daily life, periodic signals from our environment entrain our rhythms to 24 hours. But if such a signal is given once every 25 hours to an animal in an otherwise constant environment, the animal's internal rhythms will be entrained to 25 hours.

The Clock-in-a-Dish

For our group of sleepwatchers at Stanford, research on the biological clock and its role in the timing of sleep is currently the most exciting and multifaceted of our endeavors. It is likely that before the turn of the century, the clock's molecular mechanism will be largely understood.

One of our tools is an approach to brain function called tissue-slice preparation, which allows direct manipulation of critical areas of the brain. Because animals' brains are protected by a so-called blood/brain barrier, intravenously administered chemicals frequently fail to reach their targets; or, if they do enter the brain, they affect many areas at once in a confusing array.

Tissue-slice preparation, on the other hand, allows direct perfusion of specific target areas. With microelectrodes and other detection techniques, the responses of clock cells to chemical or electrical stimulation can be measured. In 1988, Joe Miller and Rebecca Prosser in our laboratory succeeded in developing a "clock-in-a-dish"—one of the very few tissue-slice preparations in the United States for the direct study of the biological clock. Just as we might remove the covers, hands, and face from an old-fashioned timepiece to examine its workings, we are now able to study the biological clock similarly removed from its casing. We often think of our clock-in-a-dish in terms of the old Timex wristwatch commercial slogan: "It takes a lickin' but it keeps on tickin'."

A major thrust of our research has been finding ways to reset this clock. Miller and Prosser have been bathing it with various compounds to see what might turn it ahead or backward. For many years, it had been thought that the biological clock was immune to most external influences—otherwise, how could it be a reliable timepiece? However, some chemicals did turn out to affect the clock's period, its amplitude, or its phase—the time at which it is set. In 1985 Fred Turek, a neurobiologist at Northwestern University, and his colleagues discovered that triazolam, the widely prescribed sleeping pill mentioned in the previous chapter, would reset the biological clock in the hamster. Strangely enough, triazolam did not put the hamster to sleep, but rather seemed to stimulate increased activity.

By bathing the clock with chemicals—mostly compounds that react with nerve-cell receptors—and measuring its phase by meticulously following the cyclic changes of its cellular firing or metabolic activity, Prosser and Miller have discovered new classes of clock-resetting compounds. The most notable are related to serotonin, a well-known neurotransmitter chemical located throughout the brain but not previously known to be involved in resetting the clock.

There is also evidence that a compound called melatonin, produced naturally in tiny amounts by the pineal gland, resets the human clock. Whereas many substances must be administered intravenously to avoid the havoc that the digestive system wreaks on them, melatonin seems to function even when taken orally. Genetic engineering may make it possible to produce melatonin in volume. I believe we are only a year or two away from a potent and safe jet-lag pill—something you could take at the beginning of a trip in order to arrive at your destination with your biological clock running at local time.

When the Clock Runs Too Slow or Too Fast

The biological clock has significance for more than jet lag; it is also the culprit in certain sleep disorders. It is part of American folklore (and questionnaire data have shown it to be generally true) that young people like to stay up late at night and sleep late in the morning, whereas senior citizens prefer to go to bed early and get up early. The former have been dubbed *owls* and the latter *larks*. In fact, the biological clock in young people has a tendency to run slow, while in older individuals it tends to run fast.

Because the natural period of the human clock is longer than 24 hours, there is a built-in tendency toward a delayed sleep phase, and the clock therefore has to reset itself each day by advancing its time approximately one hour. Thus, among high school and college students, the delayed sleep phase syndrome is commonplace. This also explains the "Sunday night insomnia"—very common among the young but afflicting other ages as well—that comes from staying up late on Friday and Saturday nights to socialize, followed by sleeping in on Saturday and Sunday mornings to compensate. Given this pattern, it's then nearly impossible to fall asleep early enough on Sunday night to get adequate sleep before it's time to get up and go to work or school on Monday.

In the 1970s, working at our then newly established sleep disorders clinic, I would occasionally see young students with profound insomnia, which they would generally characterize as "lying awake in bed with my mind racing." I eventually summoned the wit to start asking, "And what happens in the morning?" The answer was typically, "I can't get out of bed. I can't wake up." Our first case of this type was a senior in high school. Although I suspected that his biological clock was out of sync with the daily schedule he was trying to follow, I had no idea at the time what could be done about it—beyond a rigidly enforced regimen of getting up each morning with the aid of his parents, who would literally throw him out of bed.

Then early in 1976 a patient came to the clinic with a highly disruptive manifestation of this same problem. He could not fall asleep at night, and was wide awake from midnight to at least 5 or 6am and often later. He was never able to get out of bed before noon, and usually not until mid-afternoon. A graduate student in physics, this night owl had not seen his professor—a lark—all year. I felt sure this was a biological clock problem and called in Chuck Czeisler, who had come to our lab as a Stanford medical student in 1974 and was now our resident expert in such matters. We decided to attack the problem with a hitherto untried and totally unconventional therapeutic technique that would later be termed *chronotherapy.*

The idea was this: Since the natural period of the human clock was closer to 25 than 24 hours, we determined to put the student on a 26- or 27-hour day and have him go to sleep progressively later each day. Eventually his internal circadian sleep period would come back into synchrony with the natural 24-hour environmental pattern, and he could start getting up in the morning to meet with his professor. So that the therapy would not interfere with the patient's life any more than necessary, we decided to stage it during the Stanford Summer Sleep Camp.

We knew that the student fell asleep reasonably quickly when he went to bed at 6am, so this is where we started. After a full eight hours of sleep, he got up at 2pm the next day and remained awake for eighteen hours. He then went to bed at 9am, awoke at 5pm, stayed up until noon the next day, woke up at 8pm, and so on, until he reached the point where he went to bed at 9pm and fell asleep quickly. The next day we decided to set his bedtime at 10pm and freeze it right there. It worked perfectly; he stayed in sync with the earth's 24-hour cycle after that.

We named this problem delayed sleep phase syndrome (DSPS), and Chuck Czeisler developed a theoretical explanation. The biological clock of a patient with DSPS could be delayed but had a defective ability to advance, so that once a major delay occurred, it was not possible for the patient to adjust backward to a normal schedule. Czeisler, along with Elliot Weitzman, working in our lab on sabbatical from Montefiore Medical School in the Bronx, later studied additional patients who had this problem and treated them successfully with chronotherapy.

Because the free-running period of the clock is longer than 24 hours, chronotherapy in the opposite direction—trying to shorten the period—does not work as well. Fortunately, another form of treatment has become available—bright light therapy. Although light had been known as an effective clock-setting signal for animals for many years, early research showed that humans did not have the same sensitivity to light. As it turns out, this was because scientists conducted most of their studies with relatively dim light. Recently Czeisler, now a professor at Harvard with his own sleep laboratory, Al Lewy of the Health Sciences University at Portland, Oregon, and others have shown that the human clock responds strongly to bright light—the levels typically encountered outdoors during the daytime. Just as in most other organisms, light is a powerful clock-setting signal for humans.

Before the discovery that bright light would reset the human biological clock, another individual had come to our clinic with a problem similar to that of the student who couldn't sleep at night and couldn't get up in the morning. The problem, which we identified during the winter, had improved of its own accord by the time the summer came. This patient gave a history, the significance of which we did not understand at the time, of sleeping outside so that the morning sun shone brightly into his eyes. In retrospect, he was essentially giving himself bright-light therapy!

In a more formal context, bright-light therapy involves carefully providing light signals at specific times to reset the clock. To do this successfully, we need to be aware that the biological clock will reset itself at some phases of its daily rhythm, but not others. For humans, clock-resetting sensitivity occurs at night, mostly during sleep. Moreover, at some times a light pulse will delay the clock; at other times, advance it. Very early in the night a pulse of light will delay the clock slightly. As the pulse of light is given later and later during the dark period, the induced delay gets larger and larger—until close to the middle of the period, when the effect changes completely. A pulse of light given *late* in the night will *advance* the clock the maximum possible. The size of the advance gradually decreases as the pulse of light is given closer and closer to daybreak.

If someone's clock is running early, so that the person feels inclined to fall asleep before the usual bedtime, the last light of the day will thus have the effect of delaying the clock, which will bring it into synchrony with external day/night. If the person's clock is running late, the first light of the morning will advance it slightly and, once again, synchronize it. If the clock is way ahead or way behind, the pulse will produce a larger phase shift; but this shift may be in the wrong direction, throwing the clock even farther off. A clock running very early, such that the day's last light fell midway through the "sleeping" phase, would become even further advanced—exactly the opposite of what was desired. Thus, the use of bright light to reset the biological clock—say, for dealing with jet lag when many time zones have been crossed—has to be very thoughtfully administered.

Bright-light therapy is a convenient first approach to either delayed or advanced sleep phase syndrome because it is relatively easy to administer. The second approach might be chronotherapy—taking advantage of the 25-hour free-running rhythm in order to gradually bring an individual back into sync with the day/night cycle. The final approach (for a desperate, wealthy person or a student with flexible hours) would be a combination of both in a specialized laboratory environment.

In the early days of studying circadian rhythms during the 1950s and 1960s, the effort to isolate human beings from all time cues bore testimony to our ignorance about the nature of biological rhythms. We feared even the subtlest of cues—for example, Elliot Weitzman had his male technicians shave at irregular intervals so that isolated subjects could not detect time cues in the length of a technician's whiskers. However, light overwhelms most other cues. Blind people are frequently found to revert to free-running 25-hour cycles without any isolation whatsoever from our 24-hour society.

Another potent clock-setting signal is exercise. In our laboratories at Stanford, Dale Edgar has demonstrated that, like light, spontaneous activity has the ability to synchronize the clock. Animals who were free-running under constant conditions were given access to a running wheel at a regular time, once every 24 hours. From this cue alone, they maintained a 24-hour rhythm of sleep and wakefulness, with peak wakefulness occurring a number of hours before access to the wheel. Someday, when its phase-shifting effects on humans are better understood, scheduled activity as well as bright light might be used to reset the biological clock. This might be the ideal approach for athletic teams who must traverse many time zones, whether traveling to international competitions or simply coast-to-coast in the United States.

Battle of the Sleep Experts

Although new approaches with bright light were being tried in 1986, the consistent success of chronotherapy gave me the confidence to undertake a task presented to me by Standley Scott, the head trainer of the Stanford Cardinal football team. That season, the regular Stanford vs. University of Arizona football game was scheduled to be played in Tokyo, Japan, in what was termed the Coca-Cola Bowl. The team was to leave San Francisco for Tokyo on Wednesday morning, November 26; the game would be played on November 30, four days later. The trainer asked if I would be willing to help the football team avoid the effects of jet lag.

Although, the previous year, we had been involved with a massive study of airline pilots and the use of chronotherapy to counteract their jet lag, the risk of being responsible—heaven forbid—for a loss by the Stanford football team in an internationally viewed game caused me some anxiety.

On the other hand, my professional image was at stake.

My colleague, Richard Coleman, and I devised a schedule for the team that would allow the biological clock to "slip" a bit each day, thus preventing the accumulation of sleep loss of four days' sleep debt—a debt big enough, perhaps, to overcome the adrenaline of the game itself. I met with the entire football team during a regular Sunday evening post-game review to discuss the procedure.

I explained that everyone going to Tokyo, including the coaches, would have to be in bed and falling asleep by 7pm Thursday night, Tokyo time. Because this would be 2am Pacific Standard Time, a three-hour delay from their usual 11pm bedtime at Stanford, they should have no trouble falling asleep. Then on Friday night, rather than going into the nightclubs, they were to go to bed at 9pm, awakening presumably around 6am Saturday; and on Saturday night they would go to bed at 11pm, their more-or-less normal bedtime, arising as usual on Sunday morning, alert and ready to play the game at 1pm Tokyo time. This schedule meant, of course, that they would miss the evening good times, but

Jet-Lag Recommendation
The Stanford Football Team Coca-Cola Bowl

Tues. 11/25	Asleep	11:00pm
Wed. 11/26	Wake Up	7:00am
	Bus Departs	7:30 am
	Leave SFO	10:00 am

(avoid dehydration on plane)
A brief (1 hr) nap before 3pm PST recommended.
No napping after 3pm PST (8am Tokyo time).

		Tokyo Time	S.F. Time(PST)
Thurs. 11/27	Arrive Tokyo	1:40pm	8:40pm
	Bus Departs	3:00pm	10:00pm
	*Outdoor light as much as possible		
	Arrive Hotel	4:30pm	11:30pm
	Meal	6-6:30pm	1-1:30am
	Asleep	7:00pm	2:00am
Fri. 11/28	Awake	4:00am	11:00 am
	*Outdoor light as much as possible		
	Asleep	9:00pm	4:00am
Sat. 11/29	Awake	6:00am	Your body is now adjusted to Tokyo Time
	Asleep	11:00pm	6:00am
Sun. 11/30	Awake	8:00am	3:00pm
	GAME	1:00pm	8:00pm

Dehydration Techniques
• Drink plenty of fluids on plane (no caffeine)
• Walk around frequently on plane, ankle flexing 5 mins per 2 hrs

Sleep Techniques
• Follow the recommended schedule and avoid naps
• Keep the room completely dark during scheduled sleep times
• Relax in the final hour before bedtime

Diet
• Avoid caffeine, tea, chocolate, coffee, colas
• Avoid spicy food before bedtime

at least they would get to see beautiful sunrises over Mt. Fuji. I warned the team members that once they started on this course, a failure to comply 100 percent could actually leave them worse off.

Two days before the team's scheduled departure, someone told me that the Arizona football team also had retained the consultation of a sleep expert. There being only a minuscule number of sleep and biological-rhythm experts in the country (and none in Tucson), I could not imagine who it might be. The advice to the Arizona football team, the rumor went, was to "tough it out"—to immediately adopt the Tokyo schedule and hope the biological clock would catch up. This international contest thus became, for me, the battle of the sleep experts.

The game, which was to begin at 8pm Stanford time, was broadcast on cable, and fortunately the son of a colleague invited us to his home in San Jose to watch it. It was an unusual football game, punctuated by the enthusiastic but indiscriminate waving of Stanford red and Arizona blue pom-poms by the largely Japanese audience. The advantage that our special jet-lag schedule was supposed to give the Stanford team was not readily apparent; for most of the game, the lead seesawed back and forth. But in the fourth quarter, senior tailback Kevin Scott returned a kickoff 88 yards for the winning touchdown. As Stanford University president Don Kennedy, who had flown in to watch from the sidelines, later reported to me, the players on the bench were saying, "Now *there's* the edge Dr. Dement gave us." Stanford eventually won a close game, 29-24.

Did the schedule make any difference? Obviously the outcome wasn't what scientists deem "statistically significant;" but it was a lot of fun, and for several years I loved recounting my tale of the "battle of the sleep experts" at every opportunity. This practice took a wry turn at the annual meeting of the American College of Neuropsychophpharmacology a year later in Washington, D.C. I was telling my story, loudly and with great dramatic embellishment, to a good friend and colleague, and I closed triumphantly: "I can't imagine who that Arizona sleep expert could be, but whoever he is, he is a dope!"

"*I* was the Arizona sleep expert," said a voice beside me.

Turning, I found myself face to face with another acquaintance and colleague, Timothy Monk, who works at the University of Pittsburgh. I had just insulted someone I thought must be 3,000 miles away, only to find him right behind me. And so I listened, my jaw slack from embarrassment and amazement, while Tim explained why he had counseled the Arizona team to simply tough it out. The coach, a friend of his, had asked for Tim's advice. "Since I couldn't get to Arizona to personally motivate the team to comply with such an odd schedule, I was afraid they wouldn't stick to it." Under the circumstances, he may well have been right.

In the fall of 1989, I got another chance to play sleep expert to a football team. My "fame" had spread to the University of Utah, where coach Jim Fassel asked me what I would recommend for his team's journey to play the University of Hawaii in Honolulu, four time zones to the west. Brimming with great confidence (understandable in light of my undefeated record), I recommended a similar schedule. Since the Utah team's practice field had lights, they could actually go on a Honolulu schedule right at home in Salt Lake City. I was not able to see the game, but in the newspaper the next day I read that the University of Hawaii had defeated the University of Utah. Greatly abashed, I called the coach to ask what had happened. He assured me that the team had no problem with jet lag, just with their defense—the final score had been 50-38.

We don't know the extent to which the stimulation—sometimes we call it adrenaline surge—of a challenge can overcome the effects of sleep loss and jet lag. While athletic events would make excellent test cases, the stakes are far too high to actually do an experiment (though, so help me, Stanford football coach Paul Wiggin was at one time actually willing to have the team stay up all night before a game to see what happened). My guess would be that severe sleep loss over a long period of time would affect the performance of even the most dedicated athletes, because sleep loss strongly undermines motivation.

Help for the Graveyard Shift

Vast numbers of shiftworkers—probably more than 20 million Americans—must periodically throw their internal clock out of synchrony with the environment. Biological rhythm research has shown ways to better schedule shiftwork; these approaches can greatly reduce its detrimental effects. Society, however, is surprisingly resistant. The conflict of social and economic forces often prevents managers from doing the right thing.

In 1984, several Stanford undergraduates and I studied 100 nurses who worked the night shift, typically four twelve-hour nights followed by three days off. Knowing what we do about the biological clock and its rhythms, we might reasonably predict that the nurses would best adapt by sticking with their working schedule even on their days off, sleeping days and remaining active at night. Appropriate lighting conditions (darkened rooms during the day, brightly lit rooms at night) might enhance their adaptation. But, also predictably, this isn't what happened. Instead, on their days off, all 100 nurses immediately reverted to being active during the day and trying to sleep at night. As a result, more than 90 of them experienced difficulty sleeping—both in the daytime when they were working nights *and* in the nighttime on their days off. Worse, 97 showed evidence of severe sleep deprivation—drowsiness, napping or falling asleep inadvertently on the job, and drinking five or more cups of coffee while at work.

In the early 1980s, Chuck Czeisler (by now at Harvard) and Richard Coleman, at the time director of our Sleep Disorders Clinic, were asked to devise a better shiftwork schedule for a large potash refinery. They based their recommendations on two principles. First, because the human biological clock has a natural period longer than 24 hours, it is easier to delay the clock than to advance it. Thus, it is relatively easy for a worker to adapt to the rotation of a shift schedule from day (8am to 4pm) to swing (4pm to midnight) to graveyard (midnight to 8am). Most industries, however, have traditionally rotated workers through shifts in the opposite direction—from day to graveyard to swing—for no reason other than that this is what was always done. The second principle is that workers need to spend sufficient time on each shift to allow their clock to adapt to the new schedule. Most industries schedule workers to put in one week on each shift, again for no good reason—just inertia.

Czeisler lengthened the schedule to three weeks per shift, with shift rotation from day to swing to graveyard. Under these conditions, worker satisfaction, sleep, and harmony at home all improved—and, more important than anything else to the company, so did potash production.

In the late 1980s Czeisler applied the same principles to the scheduling of shiftwork for the Philadelphia police force. Predictable, marked benefits were seen, including a substantial reduction in the number of police-car accidents. But even though Czeisler had designed the schedule so that no additional time or money were required, the police commissioner refused to institute the changes on a permanent basis. Bureaucrats hate change. As I write this, the City of Philadelphia is still pursuing this irrational, retrogressive course.

Further help for shiftworkers will come with the development of a simple, safe, and effective clock-resetting pill. The carefully controlled use of bright lights throughout industry could help, too, but is less reliable because we can't isolate shiftworkers from the real world, and they are likely to encounter bright lighting in the external environment at the wrong time. If we could find a way—a blood or body-temperature test, perhaps—to quickly assess the phase of an individual's biological clock, we would know instantly what to do to help that individual adapt to any work schedule.

All of these things are possible. It remains only for managers and workers to summon the resolve to make things better by using established principles of biological rhythms, and for scientists to continue doing the necessary research to discover everything possible about how the biological clock adapts to change.

The Biological Clock vs. Sleep Debt

I would now like to say a few words about a more specific role of the biological clock in the daily cycle of sleep and wakefulness. We must think of the biological clock as a time-keeping mechanism with input signals that set it to local time and output signals by which it controls and regulates other systems in the brain and body. The input signals are light, activity, and possibly blood level of melatonin; but very little is known about output pathways. Nerve fibers going from the clock to several places in the brain have been described, but that has shed no light on how things work. Recently, Dale Edgar and I have proposed a theory that goes a little further than previous notions. We postulate that the biological clock and the sleep debt, which I described in Chapter 1, oppose one another.

Two crucial findings underlie this view. The first is that if the biological clock of an experimental animal is destroyed, sleep and wakefulness lose their 24-hour periodicity and occur at all times around the clock in brief bouts— minutes as opposed to hours—with a complete disappearance of the daily period of consolidated wakefulness. It is nonetheless still possible to keep the clockless animal awake for long periods by external stimulation and then to demonstrate that sleep deprivation increases the tendency to fall asleep. The sleep drive, in other words, is in no way diminished by the loss of the clock.

The second observation came from Edgar's doctoral dissertation, a study he carried out at the University of California at Davis under the direction of Charles Fuller, in which he damaged the biological clock in squirrel monkeys. In a later analysis of the data at Stanford, we noted that this lesion resulted not only in a chaotic sleep/wake regimen but also, significantly, in a very large *decrease* in total daily wakefulness, amounting to more than four hours.

Thus, the biological clock can be regarded as an alarm clock. Our theory postulates that signals from the biological clock keep us awake during the day, and that during the time we are awake, the drive to sleep builds up. As the clock's wake-up signal wears off, the unopposed sleep drive puts us asleep and keeps us asleep through the night. Presumably, a signal from the biological clock in the morning—when our sleep debt is lowest—wakes us up and keeps us going through the day. In order to account for the midday sleepiness that is so typical of human beings, we postulate two precisely timed wake-up pulses from the clock. One, in the morning, is weak but effective because the sleep drive is relatively low then. But because humans typically don't get enough sleep, the sleep debt begins to manifest itself by midday, around 2 or 3pm, at which time another, stronger signal from the clock jolts us awake for the rest of the afternoon into the evening. In young people, this afternoon signal is so strong that it frequently goes into the night.

It is obviously very important to us to find out how the biological clock produces this signal. Some exciting work has been done in other laboratories in the past year or two in which the clocks of rats are lesioned and then fetal clock cells are transplanted from other animals. This almost immediately restores the circadian rhythm of rest vs. activity, suggesting that the clock secretes an alerting compound; the rhythms are restored too soon to be adequately accounted for by the re-establishment of neural pathways.

Research on the biological clock and its input/output functions is at the cutting edge of neuroscience. Scientists in our group at Stanford and at other centers are working at the molecular-biological level, studying the role of genes in the regulatory mechanisms.

6

Am I a Butterfly? The World of Dreams

O nce I, Chuang Tzu, dreamt that I was a butterfly, a butterfly flying about, feeling that it was enjoying itself. It did not know that it was Chuang. Suddenly I awoke and was myself again, the veritable Chuang. I do not know whether it was then Chuang dreaming that he was a butterfly, or whether I am now a butterfly dreaming that it is Chuang. But between Chuang and a butterfly there must be a difference.

-Chuang Tzu, Taoist philosopher, c. 350 B.C.

Although I have never dreamed I was a butterfly or, as far as I recall, anything but myself, I have been drawn to the astonishing reality of the dream world like a moth to a flame. In fact, what led me to become a sleepwatcher in the first place had much to do with the phenomenon of dreaming and my fascination with its many aspects– above all, the fact that the brain, without the help of information from the senses, creates an entire hallucinatory world and places the self in this world with a sense of reality fully as strong as that accompanying the sojourner in the waking world.

Brain in a Bottle

Why do we experience our dreams as reality? The usual answer has been that the sleeping brain, being partly "shut down," lacks the capacity to make a judgment and thus accepts as "real" a fleeting and disorganized, indeed even incomplete, set of experiences. Now that we know the brain in REM sleep is working even harder than when it is awake, we can no longer really support the "impaired capacity" explanation. But we have as yet no other factual explanation; dreaming is another place, another world–a miracle of the sleeping mind that contemporary knowledge does not even begin to reduce to mundane neurophysiology.

For me, dreaming is the opportunity to hold a citizenship in two worlds, equally real but with differing logic and limitations. From this perspective, the dream world is as complete and richly detailed as the waking world. Many of the things going on in our bodies during REM sleep seem to replicate what would occur during an identical experience in the real world.

The dreaming brain seems to do exactly what the waking brain would do if events identical to the dream were taking place–and *more*, because it has to duplicate the sensory information provided spontaneously in the waking world as well as elaborate a response, which it does. That response travels down the spinal cord to the motor nerves. Only at this final stage is the response aborted. We occasionally see muscle twitching in specific limbs that reflect corresponding movement in a dream; sometimes, too, changes in breathing and heartbeat seem appropriate to the reported dream events. The parallels in eye movement patterns are even more striking. I've done studies in which I would awaken subjects after periods where their eye movements were almost all vertical, and the dream content would include such events as looking up in the sky at an airplane, watching leaflets fall to the ground, or watching a trapeze artist. When we are dreaming, we are fully conscious and aware of ourselves; we are oriented in time, place, and person. The dream world is a real place with real people in it. We experience a dream as real because it *is* real.

Imagine that your brain were placed in a bottle and kept alive and healthy, and that we had the power to exactly replicate, through brain activity, some period of your recent waking life. I postulate that you would exist, and you would exist *in a real world* as far as you could possibly know. Assuming that experiences in the dream world occur because of brain activity and, further, that this activity is similar to that occurring in the waking state, the miracle is how– without any help from the sense organs– the brain replicates in the dream all the sensory information that creates the world we live in when we are awake.

One could suggest that of the two modes of existence– dreaming and waking–the latter is much easier for the brain, because all the experience and organization of the sensory images are received passively. No creative effort is necessary; the major task of the brain is the elaboration of responses. This is apparently also the task in the dream world–except that, by yet another active process, these responses are blocked at the level of the spinal cord. Given that the dreaming brain must perform these remarkable contortions–creating a world, living in it, responding to it, and then carefully blocking all the responses in a manner that does not cross the threshold of awareness–it is no wonder that this dreaming brain seems to be more active than the waking brain.

Peering through the Frosted Glass

I have often wondered what the earliest cave dwellers made of these dual realities–the waking world and the world of dreams. Anthropologists have suggested that dreaming is what gave rise to the concept of the soul, or a supernatural spirit that could leave the body temporarily during sleep and permanently at death. Is it our "soul" that experiences the dream world? Although it may have seemed so in earlier ages, today the pervasive attitude toward dreams seems to be that we "know" they are not very important–certainly we quickly forget about them in almost every instance.

This imputed lack of importance is reinforced by the frosted glass that seems to lie between our sleeping and waking experience. It is widely assumed that none of us remember our dreams with the same accuracy and vividness that we remember our waking experiences. Exactly how much our dreams are blurred in the process of remembering them is still a great enigma. Describing the dream experience is roughly as difficult as if we were, in waking life, casually strolling without a care down the Champs Elysées; suddenly a raucous buzzer plucks us into another world, where, in the dim light of a dream bedroom, a shadowy figure begins a relentless interrogation about what we were just doing in that other (waking) world. We would surely forget a few things. That our memory for waking events in the waking state is superior may be an illusion.

In an experiment in 1972, James Bussel, Terry Pivik, and I asked subjects to recall their dreams. We then compared their accounts with the pattern of vertical and horizontal rapid eye movements recorded just prior to the arousal. For example, if just before being awakened by our buzzer, a subject had been dreaming that he dropped a book, we might expect that the last eye-movement patterns would have been downward. In fact, the correlation between the eye movements that might be postulated from the recalled dreams and the actual recorded eye movements was very poor, *but* significantly above chance when large numbers of instances were accumulated. The real payoff, however, was this: When we then performed exactly the same experiment on wide-awake subjects–recorded their eye movements, then suddenly interrupted them without warning and asked them to describe where they had just been looking– the correlation between the subjects' recall of what they had just seen and their measured eye-movement patterns was no better in wakefulness than in REM sleep!

The memory of waking experience is aided greatly by the reliable continuity of the waking world, which remains pretty much the same for most of us day after day after day. Much of what we remember, we have previously learned. If I walk through my office and am then asked to recall the experience, I will "remember" seeing my desk not only because I saw it, but because I have long since learned that it is always there. The hallmark of the dream world, on the other hand, is its discontinuity from night to night, dream to dream, and even moment to moment; there are no long-term memory aids when we try to recall what we have seen.

Time and money allowing, I would like some day to try the following experiment. I would invite ten students to my office one at a time, ostensibly for a tutorial session. When they arrived, they would be admitted to a large anteroom in which a complex but perfectly arranged and stereotyped drama would be enacted in exactly the same way for each student–every color would be specified, and every object would be in precisely the same place. Finally, a hidden video camera would record the scene in case the student did not remain a passive spectator.

At the end of five minutes, the student would be escorted quickly into another room and asked to report what had happened in the anteroom. The inquiry would be conducted in the same manner as when we awaken sleeping subjects from REM sleep. We would thus have a chance to observe how well a complex waking experience analogous to a dream would be recalled. How much of the activity and surroundings would be forgotten? How much not noticed? How much inaccuracy would be introduced? What things would be remembered in detail, or only vaguely? What colors would be recalled?

From the data, we could develop some sort of score that would express the degree of difference between the five minutes in the "real world" of the experimental room and the subject's recall of it. I expect that these differences would be quite large, and that differences among subjects would be equally large. I feel absolutely certain that such tests would tend to show that the dream world is equal in resolution to the real world but attenuated by the memory processes.

The circadian rhythm of wakefulness may also conspire against our accumulating an accurate introspective account of the dream world. It is the waking mind that must remember the dream, not the dreaming mind. Yet the waking functions, including recall, are best around noon and at their lowest ebb at around 3am–so how can we be expected to remember the midnight antics of the dreaming mind?

Even if there is some dream recall when we are awakened in the middle of the night, there may be reporting difficulties. I once dreamed that I was a concert pianist, playing the most incredible arpeggios as my fingers flew across the keyboard–far better than I could ever play piano in real life. I was accompanied by an entire symphony orchestra, and the music was magnificent. Suddenly I awoke–it was probably 1am. From the pinnacle of pianistic super-coordination in my dream, I was instantly switched to the absolute trough of my waking abilities. I was completely groggy. I couldn't get my eyes open. I attempted to get out of bed, but I was so clumsy I fell to the floor. I couldn't talk. I couldn't think. I could remember the dream, but I couldn't have possibly described it to anyone until the next day when my waking functions had improved sufficiently.

We might learn a great deal more about dreams if we could set up situations that greatly improved our access to the dream world. For example, suppose we were to study REM periods that occur during daytime napping or late in the sleep period, after about 6am, when the waking mind is better able to deal with the recall and description process. Or suppose we made the dream-recall task more introspective, with less emphasis on the items of content and more emphasis on the emotional nature of the experience.

Perhaps narcoleptic patients—with their unique pattern of falling immediately into REM sleep without passing through the usual non-REM stages—might be helpful in attempts to analyze the dream world. Because narcoleptics enter the dream world directly from the waking world, might they be able to carry into the sleep-onset REM period an awareness of the "real" world, along with the will to observe closely the properties of the hallucinated world, and the ability to make a valid comparison with reality? In other words, with the appropriate training or instructions, could a person enter a dream knowing that it was a dream and knowing that his or her task was to examine it? If so, we might at last gain entry to this shadowy world.

Remembrance of Things Immediately Past

Although we can probably account for less than perfect dream recall as being due to the special difficulty of the task, we must still ask if memory processes are *different* in sleep from those during wakefulness. Memory does appear to be impaired during sleep. Apparently a major change in memory processing occurs at the very moment of sleep onset—which incidentally helps explain the difficulty of capturing that moment. It is as if, at the instant sleep begins, the gate between short-term and long-term memory closes, and those waking memory traces that have not yet been transferred into the long-term vault merely fade away. The result, if one sleeps ten minutes or more, is a retrograde amnesia to the events just prior to the onset of sleep.

Some experimental data confirm this. If a bit of information is presented within a four-minute period before the onset of sleep, it cannot be retrieved after five minutes of sleep have elapsed. If, instead of sleep, a similar period of wakefulness intervenes, retrieval is nearly 100 percent. This phenomenon can be easily demonstrated in a classroom. While watching a sleepy student, the instructor makes a note of the lecture content just as the student unambiguously falls asleep. When the student is peremptorily awakened about ten minutes later and asked to relate the last thing he or she remembers, it is invariably not what was being discussed in the five to ten minutes before the hapless soul fell asleep. The memories of events just prior to falling asleep can be captured only if an awakening occurs within a few seconds to a few minutes following the moment of sleep onset.

Whether this applies to memories of the dream experience is not certain, but it seems to fit what we know about dream recall. Information introduced into short-term memory during sleep would decay fairly quickly—within five or ten minutes—after which retrieval may no longer be possible. If this is the case during REM sleep, then memory traces of dream experiences would not be transferred into long-term storage except during wakefulness. Accordingly, as we progress through a dream, perhaps only information from the immediately foregoing five to ten minutes is retrievable from short-term memory; dream experiences prior to that interval will have been erased. (The *rate* of decay may vary. Memory of color, for example, may fade more rapidly than memory of form.)

It is possible that this difficulty in remembering is a protective mechanism, to prevent dream memories from cluttering up our memories of wakefulness; obviously it could be most confusing if we were continually trying to sort out memory of all our dream experiences from all our waking memories. Once, early in my career at Stanford, I was attending a Stanford basketball game when my eye fell on Dr. Fred Behling–at that time the team surgeon–and I remembered seeing him at a lecture I had recently given. Since I had not been at Stanford very long and wanted to meet the man, I rushed up to Dr. Behling at half-time and said, "Thanks for coming to my lecture." He looked up at me with a blank stare, so I added, "On Tuesday, at the medical school." His stare remained blank. "I was in Chicago on Tuesday," he reported. My mouth dropped open, and I retreated to my seat in the stands; the memory was absolutely clear, but I can assume only that it had been a dream.

A final wild speculation: Maybe the brain has a special memory bank for dreams–a bank that is about as difficult for the waking mind to access as the other way around.

Probing the Realism of Dream Imagery

Dreams can seem perfectly real to us—so real as to sometimes cause us confusion. But what about the details of the dream world—are they in fact equal in resolution to the real world? If I look at a tree while fully awake, I am aware of an infinity of perceptual information. If I really focus on that tree, I see all the details of the real object, within the limits of the resolving power of my eyeball camera and the angle of aperture. I see the complex network of trunk and branches and countless leaves with their infinite subtle variations in shape and nuances of color. Imagine how many impulses per second must traverse my optic nerves in perfect pattern and sequence to "create" this picture!

If we see a tree in a dream, is it—or can it ever be—as complete, as detailed, as perfect as the image of a real tree? In order to answer this question, a dreamer would have to focus on the dream image (in this case, a large tree with summer foliage) long enough to examine it in the minutest detail, and then to report back to us whether there were, in fact, thousands of branches and leaves manifesting an infinite subtlety of shape and color—or if the dream image was only a rough facsimile of a tree.

Twenty years ago, we tried to see if subjects could achieve such reflective analysis in our laboratory in a state somewhat resembling the dream—deep hypnosis with suggested hallucinations. We instructed these deeply hypnotized subjects to "see" an object—a pair of shoes, for example—and to examine it very carefully, reporting to us exactly what they saw. Our subjects had no trouble focusing their attention on the specified object. But it was almost always perfectly clear from the subject's spontaneous account and responses to interrogation that the hallucinated object was almost always substantially different from its real counterpart. Often the hypnotized subject would express puzzlement over the strangely incomplete and flawed image. Such distorted images are common to imaginings that occur in the waking state, to sleep-onset imagery, and to various kinds of hallucinations, whether psychotic or drug-induced. On the other hand, we believe, the images we report ourselves to have seen in the dream world are identical to our perceptions in the real world.

Freeze-Frame Dreaming

In the waking state, a person would have no problem examining a facsimile of a tree and reporting on the deficiencies in its "treeness." Most people would probably say that such a simple act of reflection and analysis is beyond the capacity of the dreamer—that a dreamer cannot pause and reflect, but is relentlessly hustled from one dream event or scene to the next with little or no volitional control. My personal experience, however, suggests that reflection and analysis can occasionally be dreaming functions—and, further, that when these processes occur during a dream, the images stand up to a "reality check."

I recall one particular dream in which I approached the concession stand in the lobby of a movie house. The woman working behind the counter was wearing a white blouse. As I drew nearer, I noticed with some surprise two large, apparently damp, purple stains, approximately in the location of her breasts. My first thought was that she had uncapped, purple felt-tipped pens in her pockets. But on closer examination, I saw that her blouse had no pockets. Further, the stains were too circumscribed to have been accidentally splashed from without. At this point, I felt great puzzlement and fascination. The thought occurred to me that the woman might be a nursing mother with milk leakage; at the same time, even while dreaming I realized that bright purple was not the usual color of milk stains.

I knew that a prolonged close-up scrutiny of the woman's bosom might be offensive to her; but as she did not seem to notice me, I made what seemed to me a fairly lengthy visual examination of these strange stains. I was aware in the dream that this required a great mental effort, somewhat akin to holding a twelve-digit number in my mind. I noted the texture of the blouse, that the stains were almost certainly damp, and that they were in the exact location of her nipples. At this point, I had the extraordinary thought that she was a nursing mother whose breasts were not producing milk but rather grape juice or wine. (I cannot help wondering whether this would have been typical if the dreamer were French.)

In the dream I continued to stand there thinking about the possible explanation, wondering if the excessive ingestion of grape juice or wine could actually affect a mother's milk in such a way. I then decided to stifle my shyness and ask the woman if she was aware of the stains and whether she was, indeed, producing purple milk. At that moment, some other people in the lobby began to make a commotion. A concerted effort of will was required to ignore them and approach the woman behind the counter. At this instant, I woke up; immediately I wrote down the dream.

Putting aside any personal meaning, my main purpose in recounting this dream is to document an episode of prolonged reflection and analysis. My recall of the episode allows me to believe that the perceptual experience was as complete as if I had been awake. There were no flaws. The purple stains, though incongruous, were real; they were not hazy or indistinct. The fact that I seemed able to resist moving along or becoming involved in the commotion in the lobby suggests that I might have continued the investigation had I not awakened. It may be possible that the awakening itself was due, in part, to the conflict between my will to remain immobile in reflection, which implies control, and the normal dream mechanisms, which were continually introducing new content (the commotion in the lobby) and pushing my consciousness toward new dream scenes.

Admittedly, this reflective experience was somewhat unusual. While momentary reflections are not uncommon, it seems rare that the dreamer stops, or even desires, to pursue a single examination for any length of time.

If the dream world is so real, you may ask, why don't we experience more astonishment and skepticism about some of its events, as we might in the real world? There are several possible answers. First, if bizarre or astonishing events actually took place in the waking state, our response might well be quite similar to our dream response. Take my dream of the purple-stained blouse, for instance. What would I do if I were to have exactly the same encounter in the waking state? I would probably think of leaky pens and quickly reject the hypothesis of mammary wine. I would most likely look away quickly, concluding that the woman had some strange, symbolic reason for artificially staining her blouse. And surely I would be puzzled by the context—her presence in the concession, and the fact that other people didn't seem to notice anything. (Then again, as the long-popular TV program "Candid Camera" has shown repeatedly, people often refuse to notice the wildly improbable.)

A second possible answer is that the sleeping brain may be unable to analyze events at the required level of logical function. That is, while it clearly retains some logical powers, it may lack the questioning capability that would assess the validity of the unfolding events. Passively accepting the most bizarre premises, then, it churns ahead processing them as logically as is possible. A third possibility is that even though the dream world seems to fool us completely with its apparent reality, we may nonetheless know, at a subconscious level, that we are dreaming; thus we don't get excited about the strange and bizarre images we encounter.

When Do We Dream?

I am convinced of the correlation between dreaming and REM sleep; it is my opinion that the true, vivid dreams do not occur in non-REM sleep. One corroborating bit of evidence, it seems to me, is the inhibition of muscular activity during REM periods, which prevents us from acting out the movements that occur in our dreams. (In REM sleep behavior disorder, discussed in Chapter 4, this mechanism for suppression of the motor nerves is impaired, and the movements appropriate to the dream actually take place.)

To at least some extent, it is the intense elaboration of muscular activity by the brain that gives reality its feel. In REM sleep, only at the final, spinal level is our response turned off; the brain itself, for all practical purposes, is going through all the motions it would if we were awake. In non-REM sleep, however, the brain's motor cortex and other motor-related regions are not issuing commands—if they were, we would be moving around, since there is no muscular inhibition during that phase of sleep.

My stand is not universally accepted; other investigators have elicited reports from subjects awakened from both non-REM sleep and non-REM sleep onset that sound like descriptions of the fully intact dream world. However, I think these can be explained in any of several ways. It may be largely a semantic problem of defining a "dream;" perhaps the subject describing the non-REM "dream" images focuses on the wrong variables, ignoring differences in solidity, intensity, detail, and vividness while reporting that the concept and general form is the same. We also can't ignore the difficulty of clearly communicating our subjective experiences. Some experimenter bias may even come into play. Or maybe some people are just plain confused when aroused from non-REM sleep and are unable to handle a lack of structured mental experience—so they invent one.

I have always been intrigued by the subjectiveness of visual imagery and what people mean when they say that they see something "in their mind's eye." The concept took on new meaning for me when I was at Mount Sinai Hospital in New York City, where I spent several years as a research fellow between 1957 and 1962. Charles Fisher, a psychoanalyst at the hospital, was performing some experiments designed to determine whether objects freely imagined by a subject would bear any relationship to previously received "subliminal" messages. (Remember all that fuss about subliminal messages in movie theaters supposedly stampeding patrons out into the lobby to buy popcorn?)

As a volunteer subject in Fisher's experiment, I lay wide awake in the dark with my eyes closed for nearly thirty minutes, until I suddenly saw a visual image. It had the general shape of a hunting knife, but it was colored green, slightly darker than the background, which was a reddish-green. The experience was somewhat startling because the image, though fuzzy, was sharp enough to demonstrate to me that in all previous free-imagery sessions, I had really seen nothing at all; instead I had confounded abstract visual *thoughts* with visual imagery. Realizing this further convinced me of the inadequacy of language in the absence of direct experience. During the few seconds of its apparition, however, there was never any thought that the hunting knife I saw was real. While the image did unquestionably exist, I had no confusion that it might be a real knife, both because of its appearance—its unreal color, fuzzy outline, and flawed shape, and because of its context—a real knife would have to exist against a real background, not an amorphous, reddish-green limbo.

At this point, I ask two questions. First, was my greenish-hunting-knife image what some people are *calling* dreams? I think so—and it doesn't fit my definition. Second, was this hunting-knife image that I happened to see in wakefulness different from a hunting knife that I might see and even wield in the REM-sleep dream world? Again, I think so—I think a REM-sleep hunting knife would not have the distortions of my hallucinated green knife. I suggest that while all kinds of mental imagery may occur in non-REM sleep, the full-blown dream world associated with most people's REM sleep is fundamentally different.

Individual Differences

Charles Fisher and I once worked with a young woman who had unusually vivid and clear dream recall. Over the course of 100 REM awakenings, we were able to show an almost perfect correlation between the length of her reported dream and the length of the corresponding REM period, which established to our satisfaction the correspondence between dream time and real time.

No other subject ever exhibited such a remarkably complete memory for dreams. Individual differences deserve much more attention than they have received. Some people never remember dreams spontaneously; these individuals always show REM periods that are essentially normal, yet even arousing them from REM sleep may consistently fail to elicit dream recall. Is dreaming totally absent in these persons? Can we have one human being who inhabits the dream world every night and another who is always denied entrance? Is it possible that for some people, the dream world never exists, or exists only on certain nights?

And what about REM vs. non-REM "dreams?" Is it really possible that for some people, the dream world comes alive always and only during REM sleep, while for others it comes alive, or partially so, during non-REM sleep? Is it even possible that for some people, the state during which dreaming occurs changes from night to night? Dream-recall experiments strongly suggest that some individual differences do exist; not least among these differences are those in the typical content of people's dreams. However, there has never been enough time or money for adequate exploration of this issue, since the studies would necessarily involve hundreds and perhaps even thousands of subjects.

Since brain activity during REM sleep is substantially different from that of non-REM sleep, it's hard for me to imagine that the mental activity during these two states is not equally different. I believe that REM sleep is psychologically unique, that the neurophysiological activity taking place during the REM period gives rise to a dream world indistinguishable from the real world—except analytically and retrospectively, from the vantage point of wakefulness. The subjective experience associated with REM sleep has the quality of being real and complete. Rather than assume that for many persons this is not true, I prefer to invoke individual differences in memory processes. In the act of remembering, the full intensity and detail of the dream experience is, to a greater or lesser extent, lost or diminished. Thus non-REM and REM experiences *as recalled and described* become spuriously similar.

Do differences in dream recall correlate with individual differences in brain activity? Interestingly, there are hints of a relationship with certain psychological characteristics. People who are repressed, very tight about baring their souls, have trouble recalling and reporting dreams; those who are more uninhibited, more open, appear to have a somewhat better ability to remember their dream life. We must acknowledge that many of our assumptions about the neurophysiology of REM vs. non-REM sleep are mainly interpretive and largely unsubstantiated. Someday we may discover an as yet unspecified physiological feature of sleep that will explain the differences among individuals.

Dreams: What Do They "Mean?"

A recent popular theory about the construction of dreams, called the "activation-synthesis" hypothesis, has been proposed by J. Allan Hobson and Robert McCarley, two Harvard psychiatrists who are also eminent sleep researchers and neurophysiologists. Their studies of sleeping cats have shown that dramatic but very regular and stereotyped bursts of nerve-cell activity, apparently generated low in the brainstem, occur regularly during REM sleep. These bursts are like explosions that, flooding the sensory pathways, activate the brain and disrupt any continuity of its functioning. Hobson and McCarley feel that the dream occurs when the activated brain attempts to make sense out of this meaningless but very intense activity.

These investigators have concluded that the brain in REM sleep (like the brain in waking) has the task of achieving a meaningful integration of sensory data even if it must resort to create its own story. The meaning of dreams, for those who support the activation-synthesis hypothesis, is accordingly transparent rather than opaque. The superficial content of dreams *is* the content of dreams; there is no need for deciphering. Since the dream state occurs in the brain of an individual, dreams are likely to reveal that particular person's specific cognitive styles, projected view of the world, and specific historical experiences. The notion that dream meaning is hidden and disguised is thus no longer either necessary or sufficient to account for the meaning of dreams. The same dream image can mean different things to different people, as opposed to the psychoanalytic practice of reducing many symbols to one or two instinctual drives or to sexual anatomy.

Those who know something about the history of psychoanalysis may well imagine the stir this heretical view of dreaming has caused. Even as Freud and his theories have faded from center stage, there is a feeling—partly from inertia, and perhaps partly from an archetypal awareness—that dreams do have some profound message for us. Of course, with twenty to thirty profound messages per night, we could spend all the next day just sorting them out. At any rate, the overt experience of the dream is often so absurd— the story so confusing—that we look for some hidden meaning.

Interpreting dreams is very much like discriminating between the deed and the motive in real life. The politician feeds the hungry. Is he genuinely concerned and humanitarian, or merely buying votes, or both? Will we ever know? In any case, the controversy that has existed since dreams were first taken seriously continues unabated. Are they purposeful and meaningful, or are they generated and influenced largely by random processes in the brain during REM sleep?

Here the commonly used terminology causes some confusion. We must distinguish between *meaning* and *purpose;* while something cannot be both random and purposeful, it *can* be both random and meaningful. If you were gazing up at the clouds and, for just a moment, the random formation seemed to suggest a face, then that face would have *meaning* for you, the person who saw it. If the face stimulated a memory of your father, it might be even more meaningful. However, it would be totally absurd to say the clouds *purposefully* took that formation so that you would have the experience of seeing a face. In the same way, a Rorschach (inkblot) card may mean one thing to one person and something else to another; it was not made for the specific purpose of causing Joe Blow to see a bat, or a blow fish, or a butterfly. If I "see" in a Rorschach card a menacing figure, I could take this as a warning of impending doom—but that is its personal meaning for me, not the *purpose* of the card. Similarly, if a menacing figure appears in a dream because of a random process, then it cannot have the purpose of warning us about anything; nevertheless, we can still look at the dream and find meaning in the same way we would find personal meaning in a movie, a painting, a musical work.

Dr. Dement's Drug-Induced Dream

Regardless of the semantics, I disagree with the random-process theory; I cannot accept that the creation of the dream is a product of chance. Tell me if you think this next dream—one of my personal favorites—was random. It dates back to 1968, when my colleagues at Stanford and I were working with PCPA, an experimental drug that appeared to have profound effects upon the basic sleep processes. We were working with furious intensity to study all the changes. About one year into the project, I developed a serious suspicion that the chemical we had been purchasing from a manufacturer was not PCPA, but something else. I experienced tremendous uneasiness. Was the rug about to be pulled out from under us? Would a whole year of work go down the tubes? I resolved to get samples of the compound analyzed in a lab; but the weekend was approaching, so nothing could be done until the following Monday. I could only wait and hope I was wrong.

Friday afternoon I went to a party at the home of artist and Stanford professor Nathan Oliveira. He was talking about a recent trip to Sweden, where he had had a show. During this trip, he said someone had asked him if he was Jewish (he is, in fact, Portuguese), and he responded in jest, "There are no Jews in Portugal."

That night I had a lengthy, vivid dream. It took its theme from the movie *Around the World in 80 Days* and from the day's events. In this dream, I was on the trail of the lost tribe of Portuguese Jews. I would pursue them over mountain and plain and arrive at the warm ashes of a campfire, only to realize that the lost tribe was still ahead of me. With considerable intensity, I followed them across the United States, across the Atlantic Ocean, across Europe and Asia—always arriving, after considerable hardship, a little too late. Eventually I got to Vladivostok, where, upon learning they had sailed for California, I requisitioned a boat and set out to sea.

There were raging storms, and toward the end of the voyage the boat sank. Buffeted by waves, I struggled through the surf and was finally thrown up onto a California beach, totally exhausted and bereft of everything. As I crawled up on the sand totally defeated, my head bumped something. It was a signpost. I looked up and read on the sign: "Ha, ha! We were here all the time! (Signed,) The Portuguese Jews." I awoke with a feeling of overwhelming loss and failure.

Certainly the dream was humorous, at least in retrospect, but what did it "mean?" To me it clearly depicted the fear that we had gone all the way around the world—that is, had worked a whole year—and had accomplished absolutely nothing. It reflected the intensity of the work and, at the end, a tremendous sense of loss and waste. (As it turned out, my harrowing world tour was unnecessary—lab results on Monday showed that the PCPA was, in fact,

PCPA.) Its significance aside, the dream was a coherent and meaningful whole. How could it possibly have occurred as a random process?

Sigmund Freud offered a second possibility—that dreams reveal the workings of the subconscious mind. I do not want to dismiss his dream theory out of hand, but unfortunately it is extraordinarily difficult to devise experiments to test Freud's theoretical structure. "Forbidden impulses" are postulated but difficult to demonstrate. They are, by definition, disguised as they intrude on the dream scenario. They can supposedly be revealed through the method of "free association," but that method is by its very nature uncontrolled.

Aha! Dreaming About Sex?

Society's veneration of Freud died away in the 1960s, but his legacy to our time includes the persistence of the popular belief that no matter what you dream about, you are dreaming about sex. Entire books of "dream symbols" help you translate nearly every element into a sexual symbol. The connection between dreams and sex may seem indisputable to some, but a fundamental principle of science is that things are not always what they appear to be.

Take the penis for example.

Upon being asked for the umpteenth time, "Where do dreams come from?" one of my sleepwatcher colleagues answered, with a straight face, "I don't know, but I think the erect penis is the antenna that captures the signal." He was referring to a remarkable concomitant of REM sleep; namely, throbbing penile erections. If you were interested in observing REM periods among male sleepers, you would not need a polysomnographic hookup, but could simply watch the penis. When the size increased sharply, you would know that REM sleep was occurring (unless, of course, the individual was *not* asleep and was having a waking sexual fantasy.)

The regular rhythmic occurrence of nighttime penile erections was reported by German investigators in 1944, but this observation went no further until it was rediscovered independently by John Karacan at New York University's Downstate Medical Center in Brooklyn and by Charles Fisher at Mount Sinai Hospital in Manhattan. Both were monitoring subjects all night long via EEG recordings, and as one measure of physiological function, they wrapped an air-inflated rubber doughnut around the penis. When tumescence occurred, the pressure change was noted. These investigators quickly realized that REM periods were, almost without exception, associated with erections—or what we now call (in our inimitable scientific fashion) *nocturnal penile tumescence* (NPT). The same phenomenon has been observed in male dogs, cats, and rats, in case you wanted to know.

Although NPT might suggest that Freud was right—that hidden sexual impulses are present in most, if not all dreams—the content of dreaming rarely bears any relation to this sexual activation. A newborn baby boy, on his first day of life, has an erect penis whenever REM sleep occurs. His penis is therefore erect nearly eight hours a day, though he can hardly be dreaming of having sex. While little data exist, general observations suggest that the nearly 100 percent association of REM sleep with NPT continues from infancy to adolescence, when the phenomenon of wet dreams (nocturnal emissions) begins and becomes fairly prevalent. These emissions are almost always associated with erotic dream content, but NPT itself is not. Occasionally, NPT is seen during non-REM sleep—and more frequently, according to Karacan, if REM periods are eliminated.

Most investigators today feel that NPT represents a visible manifestation, along with accelerated breathing and heart rates, of non-specific activation of the autonomic nervous system during REM sleep. That is, REM sleep is simply a time of spontaneous arousal in males; just as rapid eye movements characterize REM sleep, so do penile erections. The only particular relationship to dream content was shown by Charles Fisher, who found that when dreams become anxious or nightmarish and unpleasant, the penis often shrivels.

Years ago a woman came to consult me, reporting that her husband was constantly dreaming about sex with other women—as evidenced by his repeated throbbing erections throughout the night. She was worried that this was the result of infidelity in real life. I was able to dissolve her fears, assuring her that the NPT she was witnessing had no sexual significance whatsoever, and advising her to forget about it—or, if she chose, to take advantage of it for her own pleasure.

Is there a comparable sexual arousal in females? This is not something I have ever studied myself—although somewhere out there is a Catholic nun who might harbor a few suspicions. A sufferer of sleep apnea, she had undergone testing at our Sleep Disorders Clinic. Owing to some confusion in the billing office, she (and countless other patients, I must add) received a bill for the wrong test. We didn't know what had happened until we received an irate call from this nun. Her bill was for NPT testing, and having just found out what the letters stood for, she was damned if she was going to pay.

In any event, the question of REM-related sexual arousal in females remains unsettled because no valid physiological measurement has yet been widely accepted. Several investigators have reported that REM periods are associated with increased vaginal blood flow. However, the findings seem to be much less consistent than in males. This may reflect the general tendency of males to be more easily aroused than females, and perhaps more sexually aggressive as well.

There is no doubt that people of both sexes do experience dreams with vivid sexual content. In fact, dream-content reports suggest that the inhibitions of wakefulness are weakened in dreams. Thus both men and women have reported dreams of sexual intercourse with dogs, horses, and other animals. This should not be taken as a sign of anything; totally normal people may dream of committing murder. Such dreams do not reflect upon the dreamer's waking personality.

In our labs, we have noticed an increase in sexual fantasies among human subjects who were being REM-deprived. This suggests that REM sleep, and perhaps the concurrent dream world activities, serve to release sexual tension. Patricia Garfield, a private counselor, has written extensively about dreaming. The title of Garfield's book *Pathway to Ecstasy* refers to the author's claim that she can dream to orgasm several times every night. In this day of AIDS, when promiscuous, frequent sexual encounters are undoubtedly on the wane in the general population, it may be that bottled-up sexual urges could be discharged in dreams—the safest of "safe sex" practices. This raises two questions. If someone were sexually frustrated in the waking state, and had sexual dreams that included orgasm and were "satisfying" but were not remembered in the waking state, would such dreams satisfy a person's urges? And, if someone dreamed to orgasm several times every night and *remembered* it, would that person have more or less sexual desire in the daytime? I do not know the answer to either question, but, at least in the second case, I suppose most of us would be willing to give it a try.

Or maybe I should say "most of us males," for there does seem to be a distinct gender difference in dreaming preferences. In my undergraduate "Sleep and Dreams" course, I often ask "If you could control your dreams, what would you most like to dream about?" More than 95 percent of the males answer "Having sex," while only 5 percent of the females give this blunt answer, preferring "Adventure," "Romance," and "Having a family," among a host of other things.

It is a most entertaining parlor game to ask people that question—If you could absolutely control your dreams, without losing the sense of reality, what would you choose to dream about? Would I, for instance, amass great wealth, dine at Grand Vefour, dance like Nijinsky, sing like Caruso, sleep with Marilyn Monroe, quarterback the Chicago Bears, explore the universes? But then, we so often forget our dreams—would we not need to remember and savor such experiences in the waking state in order for them to be psychologically fulfilling and rewarding? We may have had the greatest triumphs and conquests in our dreams last night, but because they are forgotten, we may still feel timid and ineffectual today.

Lucid Dreaming:
Taking Charge of the Nighttime World

Controlling your dreams may sound like the stuff of science fiction, but in fact it is fast becoming reality through the phenomenon of lucid dreaming. My first encounter with lucid dreaming occurred in the late 1970s when I was approached by a Stanford graduate student in psychology, Stephen LaBerge, who wanted to use our sleep laboratory facilities to study a phenomenon that he himself commonly experienced—knowing you are dreaming *while* you are dreaming. LaBerge was interested in trying to find out if lucid dreaming actually occurred during REM sleep or at some other time; he also wondered if lucid dreaming had any physiological markers. I had read a book called *Studies in Dreams* by Mary Arnold-Forster, published in 1921. As I recall the book, it was essentially a diary of this researcher's dream adventures. She often knew when she was dreaming and had learned to "control" her dream life, deliberately undertaking such nocturnal adventures as a trip around the world and making conscious decisions about where to travel in her dreams.

I was a little skeptical about this woman's accounts and, similarly, a little skeptical about Steve LaBerge's proposal. However, we quickly designed an experiment to prove whether lucid dreaming occurred during REM sleep. The plan was to record Steve in the sleep laboratory. If he realized he was dreaming and continued to dream, he would give us a previously-agreed-upon signal; that is, he would look right and left in a prearranged pattern. When the technician saw this pattern, he would awaken LaBerge and elicit his dream experience. There would also be awakenings when the signal did not occur.

We found perfect correspondence and, by 1980, had compiled enough data to prove that in lucid dreaming, the dreamer indeed became conscious of being in the dream world, could remain in the dream world, and could, from that vantage point, communicate with the outside world. The possibilities were exciting. Now, at last, it seemed that people might be able to use the dream world for their own purposes—for breathtaking adventures, for practicing the piano, or for almost anything. Further, it would be extremely interesting to live in the dream world and communicate continuously with the outside world. Surely, our ingenuity could devise many ways to do this.

Though we applied for a number of grants to continue our study of this phenomenon, all were rejected. Unfortunately, the discovery had come at the end of a long decline of interest in dream research or psychoanalytic interpretation of dreams—and, in general, any interest at all in the sleeping brain. Nonetheless, Dr. LaBerge has continued his work, often under extraordinarily difficult circumstances—supported largely through private donations (by no means a large sum) from interested individuals.

Large population surveys suggest that about one person in five recalls having at least one dream in which they knew they were dreaming. Only a relatively small percentage of the population has this experience frequently. Much of LaBerge's work in the past decade has been directed toward finding ways to teach people to dream lucidly. He has succeeded in devising some ingenious techniques; his latest effort is a comfortable mask that anyone can wear at home. The mask and accompanying tiny computers will detect rapid eye movements and respond at some interval by flashing tiny lights into the eyes with a beam that traverses the closed eyelids. If the dreamer becomes aware of flickering illumination, it will trigger a memory that this was to happen in the dream; with this realization the dream becomes lucid.

While many people have had the experience of realizing a dream is a dream, this almost always coincides with waking up. The following is an example of a genuine lucid dream in which the dreamer carries on in full awareness of the situation for some time:

> I was, I thought, standing in my study; but I observed that the furniture had not its usual distinctness—that everything was blurred and somehow evaded a direct gaze. It struck me that this must be because I was *dreaming*. This was a great delight to me, as giving the opportunity of experimentation. I made a strong effort to keep calm, knowing the risk of waking. I wanted most of all to see and speak to somebody to see whether they were like the real persons, and how they behaved. I remembered that my wife and children were away at the time (which was true), and I did not reason to the effect that they might be present in a dream, though absent from home in reality. I therefore wished to see one of the servants; but I was afraid to ring the bell, lest the shock would wake me. I very cautiously walked downstairs—after calculating that I should be more sure to find someone in the pantry or kitchen than in a

workroom, where I first thought of going. As I walked downstairs I looked carefully at the stair-carpet, to see whether I could visualize better in dream than in waking life. I found that this was *not* so; the dream carpet was not like what I knew it in truth to be; rather, it was a thin, ragged carpet, apparently vaguely generalized from memories of seaside lodgings. I reached the pantry door, and here again I had to stop and calm myself. The door opened and a servant appeared—quite unlike any of my own. This is all I can say, for the excitement of perceiving that I had created a new personage woke me with a shock. The dream was very clear in my mind; I was thoroughly awake; I perceived its great interest to me and I stamped it on my mind—I venture to say—almost exactly as I tell it here. (from Stephen LaBerge, *Lucid Dreaming*, New York: Ballantine, 1986).

This passage captures the uncanny sense and the sharp paradoxes of being in a completely "real" place and, at the same time, knowing that it is *not* real. It is one step beyond viewing a large screen movie; in this "movie," the observer can actually participate.

In its detail and precision, the "world" observed by the lucid dreamer is identical to real life, but with some tendency to subtle shifts. According to LaBerge, if you are looking at a book in the dream and turn your eyes away for a few moments, it is definitely not exactly the same when you look back. There remains, however, a tangible reality in the dreamer's physical reactions—insofar as they are not blocked. In laboratory studies of lucid dreaming, we have noted—and LaBerge has extended this considerably—that appropriate physiological responses occur simultaneously with the lucid dream. Thus, during an exciting moment, the heart speeds up and breathing becomes irregular. Similarly, breath-holding in a dream is associated with actual cessation of respiration in reality.

The obvious thought intrudes, What about sex? The following lucid dream is described by LaBerge:

A bizarre detail made me realize that I was dreaming. I made an eye movement signal, then proceeded through the roof, flying Superman-style. Having landed in the backyard of a house, I wished for a woman. A cute woman walked out of the patio door. We went in the backyard, and I signaled the beginning of foreplay. An instant later her blouse was on the ground and the nipples of her blossoming breasts stood out. She kneeled on the ground and began to kiss me in a most stimulating manner. I felt myself about to climax and closed my eyes in ecstasy as I had the orgasm, and again signaled. When I opened my eyes, I seemed to have awakened from a wet dream. I was very excited at the accomplishment of my experiment, then I realized it was only a false awakening, and at this I actually awoke. Although I found I had not actually ejaculated, I still felt the tingling in my spine and I marveled at the reality that the mind could create. (Ibid.)

Being aware, being conscious in our dreams is just part of lucid dreaming. Even more important is taking the next step— controlling our dreams. The ability for volitional control apparently varies from one lucid dreamer to another. If you are on a street, you cannot be totally sure what is around the corner as you walk. You can be surprised in a lucid dream, or you can create a mental attitude of expectation about something that then may actually occur. If we could gain control of the dream world, we might possess an amazing psychological resource—using our dreams to solve problems, to face and overcome fears, resolve conflicts, and otherwise stimulate personal growth. Thus, for example, if you were terribly afraid of bears, you could will yourself to dream about bears, then confront them, maybe punch them in the nose, or in some other way master them. I did something similar with tornadoes— which had inexplicably fascinated and terrified me probably ever since, as a small child, I first saw the Judy Garland classic, *The Wizard of Oz*. Anyway, I once dreamed that I fired a cannon at a tornado and dissipated it; after that dream, tornadoes ceased to have much interest for me.

131

I do wonder, though, whether we might also lose some element of this tremendous psychological resource if we were to control *all* our dreams. In *Some Must Watch While Some Must Sleep*, I reported a dream that I am convinced saved my life. It involved the discovery that I had inoperable lung cancer and little time left to live. Upon waking, I felt an exquisite joy and relief that it was just a dream—and I immediately quit smoking. Now suppose that I had undertaken such a dream volitionally. Would it have had the same emotional impact if I knew that it was a dream? It is difficult to imagine that it would.

And while I know that lucid dreaming has much to offer, I also wonder what would happen if someone became lucid *without* realizing that the dream world was a dream— or in some way began to doubt the reality of the world. This has apparently not happened to anyone, but it has been the subject of one episode of the television series *The Twilight Zone*: A woman awakens from a dream only to find that she is still in the dream—but now she is not sure. Perhaps something like this happens occasionally in the psychotic state.

Pioneer Explorers

Although dream research, and particularly research on lucid dreaming, has continued to remain outside the mainstream, there is now a professional society, the Association for the Study of Dreaming, with its own journal entitled *Dreaming*. LaBerge, a leading light in the field, is himself president of The Lucidity Institute, a Portola Valley, California based membership organization for people interested in helping to advance research in this area. The Institute offers courses on lucid dreaming and attempts to show individuals how this capacity can be learned.

Dream research should be an exciting frontier. It is sad, indeed, that the field is not regarded as more respectable by the scientific community. It is possible to greatly prolong

REM sleep in cats by injecting certain chemicals into a tiny brainstem area. I see no reason why this might not be possible in human beings in the future. It might benefit individuals who are severely maimed or crippled or quadriplegic—they might choose to spend more time in the dream world, where, with bodies made whole again, they could engage in pleasurable activities denied them in the real world. The first episode of the extraordinarily popular television series *Star Trek* involved a similar situation. Mr. Spock was returning his previous captain, who had been completely paralyzed by an accident (he could signal yes or no with his brain waves), to a world in which the mental powers of the inhabitants were able to create an hallucinatory virtual world in which the captain might live a fuller life for the remainder of his days.

We come, once again, to the question of why human beings have REM sleep, and why the human brain has the capacity to create an almost completely real world—certainly, a world with sufficient reality for our totally committed participation. If we look for the function of our dreaming, here and now, there are not many satisfying hypotheses that accord sufficient importance to the phenomenon. However, if we could truly learn to become aware of and control our dreams, they could have an enormous variety of uses.

The final possibility—which I mentioned with great hesitation because it involves another even more outlandish assumption—is that dreams are really for the future. As an extension of lucid dreaming, a special function might enable the dreamer to use the nighttime world to experience alternatives as completely as possible in the flesh, so to speak. Do you want to live in Northern Canada or in Central America? You could try living in both places in the dream world, and you might thereby discover something that would make the choice easy and definitive. Or perhaps you are in love with two partners and cannot decide which to marry. You could dream of being married to each, and perhaps both the experience itself and some hidden wisdom of the brain would foster the right decision. In this sense, maybe the dream world connects directly to what we call intuition.

Is lucid dreaming a capacity that human beings once had and then lost? Michel Jouvet, France's most prominent sleep researcher, had a notion like this. He studied 5,000 of his own dreams—not lucid—and whenever he traveled to a different country or a place far removed from his home, he found that he would dream of home for at least eight days. Accordingly, he hypothesized that one original function of the dream was to enable primitive people to find their way back to the home cave, or at least to be reminded of home so they would be motivated to return safely to it.

Maybe in the Space Age, the dream world will help us prepare for the alien realities we will encounter when we eventually travel among the stars.

7

Sex, Drugs, Rock 'n' Roll, and High Anxiety: The Scientific Life

Dement, you'd REM-deprive your own mother.

—One sleepwatcher to another

Well, maybe I would, and maybe I wouldn't. But one thing is for sure: Scientists—and especially sleepwatchers—are not quite like everyone else. Put it this way. If you got a bunch of us together for a flag football game with $500 riding on the outcome, and the final score was 6-0, the losers would refuse to pay up because the score "wasn't statistically significant." We bring to our outlook on life an odd mix of detachment, caution, and precision that is little appreciated—least of all by the media, who want flashy figures and dramatic stories to grab the public's attention.

There is also a certain mystique about the scientific life; perhaps because so many scientists move in the ethereal (if not incomprehensible) realms of mathematics and physics, their lives and their work seem almost sacrosanct. For that very reason, I think, the media are sometimes overzealous in an effort to find the human interest side of every scientific story. Reporters ask all kinds of crazy questions, some of which can't be answered and many of which shouldn't be. Even though the domain of a sleepwatcher is about as down-to-earth as science ever gets, I have not been exempt from a reporter's assiduous probing. In fact, those of us in sleep research may be more vulnerable than most, given the high association between the household bed and sex—the most common euphemism for sexual intercourse is "to sleep with." We should keep this in mind during our encounters with the press. Sometimes we learn the hard way.

Sex in the Afternoon

In September 1970, I invited a reporter from the *San Francisco Chronicle* to come visit us and get the story on the brand-new and first-ever Sleep Disorders Clinic at Stanford University. For nearly two hours, the reporter inspected our facilities and asked all the right questions—What did we plan to do? Who would be our clientele? What did we hope to learn? Pleased by the interview, I was feeling expansive when, toward the end, the reporter said he wanted to ask a few questions "off the record"—a phrase that should put anyone on guard— "just to satisfy my own curiosity." Then he asked me, "Should young children sleep with their parents?"

Certainly this issue had never been the subject of any of my sleep research, it being more in the realm of child psychology. But, hesitant though I was to stick my nose into a hornet's nest of conflicting ideas on child-rearing practices, I did have an opinion, and I stated it. It made no sense to me, I said, to isolate an infant or small child just for the convenience of the parents. The image of a little one awakening from a nightmare and being forced to suffer its terrors alone in a darkened room simply seems wrong—always has, always will.

Not only should young children not be prohibited from sleeping with their parents, I averred, but there should be no reluctance about bringing them into the comfort and warmth of the parental bed any time they are fearful or simply didn't want to sleep alone. "Above all," I added, "there should never be a major confrontation over this issue. I don't believe it does any harm whatsoever to the child or children. I even know people who add a dog or two."

Then the reporter asked the inevitable question: "Well, what about sex?"

"I don't believe," I replied staunchly, "that parents should ever have sexual intercourse in the presence of small children, but it wouldn't take too much creativity to think about having sex somewhere else, or even having one room for sex and another room for sleep. Why, it might even be better," I continued, warming to my subject, "to have sex much more often in the daytime, when the children are at school or napping!" I explained that there was some evidence that the circadian sexual rhythm might actually peak in the daytime.

I went on and on. At some point the reporter began to seem a little too interested, and I noticed he was taking notes. "This is off the record, isn't it?" I reminded him. "Oh, yes," he nodded.

About two weeks later I was awakened while it was still dark by a ringing telephone. "This is CBS Radio, New York City," said the voice. "Can we talk to you a few minutes?"

"Good heavens, it's 5am," I said, and hung up. I went back to bed, but as I was starting to drift off it came to me in a blinding flash. "Oh, no—it must have been a slow news day!"

I ran outside to retrieve the morning paper, and there on Page One was the headline: "Stanford Professor Recommends Communal Sleeping." I turned on the radio, and before too long I heard someone saying, "That's the way they do it down on the Farm, ladies and gentlemen." Not only had the story appeared in the *Chronicle*, it had gone out over the wires, and it was very embarrassing—particularly the part about Professor Dement enjoying sex in the afternoon.

Thanks to some fancy footwork by my friend the late Bob Lindee, then associate dean of the Stanford Medical School, the local *Palo Alto Times* dropped the story, and by noon it was no longer on the local airwaves. Still, every time I went outdoors I felt as if everyone was staring at me and whispering, "Isn't that the one?" Worse yet, this flap occurred just a few days before my wife and I were to move into a freshman dormitory as faculty residents, whose first responsibility is to set good examples for the students. I started feeling better, finally, when one of our older student assistants mentioned that he had read the news story and thought it was "totally cool."

Several Rockettes and One Suspicious Film Canister

While the unenlightened may harbor sleazy fantasies about sleep laboratories, the reality is that the highest standards of behavior must be, and are, upheld—if only to stem the tide of innuendo about what we are *really* doing.

In the early days of sleep research, there was a *de facto* prohibition against studying either female subjects or sexual functions during sleep, although the "wet dream," or nocturnal orgasm, was of some interest in its physiological connection to the sleeping brain. In 1954, while working in Nathaniel Kleitman's lab, my curiosity about whether rapid eye movements during sleep occurred in females as well as males led me to suggest recording the sleep of a female subject. Kleitman was definitely against it; he grumbled and muttered about our vulnerability to scandal, how I could ruin my career, and so forth. Finally he consented to letting me study my own very trustworthy girlfriend, but only in the presence of a chaperone. For this job he designated my fellow lab researcher Eugene Aserinsky, who would appear in the evening and promptly fall asleep on a cot in another room while I satisfied my urge to observe typical periods of rapid eye movement in a young woman all night long.

Though the propriety of our work was beyond reproach, I took a step in 1959 that was to raise a few eyebrows. That year, while I was living (now married) in New York City and working as a part-time resident and research fellow at Mt. Sinai Hospital, I wrote a grant proposal in which I asked the government to pay the rent of a personal apartment that I would convert to half-laboratory, half-home. (I neither sought nor obtained institutional approval for this grant.) This way I could do all-night sleep recordings for many nights on end without being absent from my family. Additionally, I could easily become the subject myself, with family members, friends, or colleagues monitoring the equipment during my daytime sleep. At the end of the '50s, the few researchers who studied human sleep were all staying up at night themselves. This apartment was therefore a tremendous boon. Furthermore, it was a cheap way to get additional laboratory space.

During this era of my apartment-based research, a Barnard student saw my newspaper advertisement for paid research subjects. She also happened to be a member of the world famous dance troupe, the Rockefeller Center "Rockettes." The notion of earning money for merely sleeping—period—was very attractive to her and to other members of the troupe. Thus began the following routine. A lovely woman, still in theatrical makeup, would arrive at the apartment building and ask the doorman for my room. In the morning she would reappear, sometimes with one of my unshaven and exhausted male colleagues who had spent the night monitoring the EEG. On day, the doorman could finally stand it no longer. "Dr. Dement," he demanded, "exactly what goes on in your apartment?" I just smiled.

There were other ramifications to an apartment laboratory, not all of them related to speculations of impropriety. One of these became apparent the night we were studying the arousal threshold of children. We had found that when children drop off to sleep after a long day of going totally flat-out, their state resembles a coma—they are extraordinarily hard to awaken and, indeed, often *cannot* be awakened. They may stand up, look around in a glazed way, make rudimentary movements, perhaps even walk through a door, but they are truly not awake. In this experiment, we were trying to rouse them with noise, and the level went higher and higher without result. The experiment was abruptly cut off by a pounding on the door, through which an outraged man from several floors below informed us in no uncertain terms that we had awakened half the building's tenants (though presumably none of the children).

Eventually one resident of the building tried to bring a lawsuit to force the laboratory out of the apartment. Fortunately, we made plans to relocate to California before the issue came to a head. On the day we left for Stanford, I found myself in the elevator with the man who had sought my ouster. I had with me my two little girls, who were coming down with chicken pox, and I couldn't resist. "Sir," I asked him, looking gently down at my daughters, "have you ever been vaccinated for smallpox?" As his gaze followed mine, his eyes widened in horror at the scrofulous pox that covered them. I hope it caused him a little anxiety.

Some years later, I had occasion to wonder if my reputation for the New York apartment and its mysterious night-time goings-on was still dogging me. I was on my way to a scientific convention in Montreal where I would be reporting on, among other things, my REM-deprivation studies. In our research, we had seen evidence of hypersexuality in human subjects who were being REM-deprived—at least we had found an increase in sexual fantasies. Our studies of cats and rats had also shown clear evidence of hypersexuality under similar conditions. These observations have long remained controversial because in cats, and to some extent dogs, a tremendous variety of situations will evoke mounting behavior. Almost everyone with a pet dog has, at one time or another, seen that dog attempt to mount the leg of a guest. Anyway, after a few days of medication with the substance PCPA, certain aspects of REM sleep began to intrude into the experimental animals' waking state, accompanied by what appeared to be hallucinatory behavior along with a dramatically increased tendency to sexually mount.

In 1968, my colleagues and I made movies of this hypersexual behavior in cats in order to provide convincing evidence for skeptical colleagues. I was taking a canister of this film with me to show at the Montreal meeting. The canister was labeled "Sex and PCPA." As I was going through customs, one of the officials laid eyes on this provocative item. I guess he thought I was some kind of sex pervert or heaven-only-knows-what, but the customs people insisted on holding me until they had viewed the film. This meant spending about half a day at the Montreal airport while they tried to locate a 16-mm movie projector. I was not exactly proved innocent—they just didn't know what to make of five cats having an orgy. As soon as I had retrieved my contraband, I immediately changed the label to "Home Movies: Children Playing Hopscotch," and put the film in the farthest reaches of my suitcase. I had no trouble getting out of Canada.

Where *Did* All That LSD End Up?

The same sort of person who winks or leers knowingly over "sleep" research probably thinks it's double the fun that, as doctors, we sleepwatchers have access to just about any drug you could name. But long before the "Just say NO" campaign, I was well educated in the hazards of drug abuse, and I've always felt a responsibility to use them with utmost caution.

In 1951, medical students could go to the pharmacy of the medical school and ask for and obtain medications— supposedly for their personal use, though this was never monitored. At the time, the most requested compounds were antibiotics, but I wanted—and got—copious supplies of barbiturates and amphetamines so I could study their effects on sleep. I told no one and asked for no one's permission—not because I was trying to hide anything, but simply because it wasn't expected. Nobody asked me; nobody said I needed any approval; in those days, that simply was the way it was.

By 1955 or '56, LSD had come upon the scene. I first became aware of it through a graduate student in the University of Chicago Department of Physiology who was doing "scientific experiments" with it; he was, from my perspective at the time, really weird. Within a year or two, while I was in New York trying to learn more about REM sleep, it occurred to me that perhaps a potent hallucinogen like LSD might have some unique effect on the dreaming brain.

To obtain the compound, I merely called Sandoz, the drug company; a day or so later, a representative appeared in the laboratory with a huge box. Inside were 1,000 vials, each containing 100 micrograms of LSD. He dropped it off without even asking for identification. No forms, no signatures, no receipts. Exercising reasonable caution, I did not use any of the drug for quite a while. I finally selected a sub-

142

ject and gave him 50 micrograms at bedtime, but nothing happened. He felt nothing, and his sleep did not change. The next night I gave him 100 micrograms; again nothing happened. "Either these vials contain water," I thought, "or there's nothing to this LSD hype." Unimpressed, I stored the drug away.

Later Howard Roffwarg, still at Columbia/Presbyterian, produced a very interesting result, which no one has ever tried to confirm. He increased REM sleep fourfold by giving low doses of LSD at bedtime. My curiosity aroused, I gave another subject 25 micrograms; he stated only that it made him feel "very uncomfortable." In 1963 I brought the supply to Stanford with me, but keeping track of it was not a high priority. When the LSD scandals broke around 1969 (it was discovered that the CIA had been secretly dosing military personnel), we attempted to go back and trace all of the supplies, and came up empty-handed. Fortunately, I had gotten mine before records of any kind were kept.

To this day, I have no idea what happened to my LSD samples. But in the intervening years, both medical schools and the drug industry have tightened up considerably. Today, in fact, the regulations surrounding the testing and marketing of a new drug are often so great as to be prohibitive; unless the potential market for a drug is up around $100 million in annual sales, a pharmaceutical company is unwilling to tackle the red tape involved in developing it. Moreover, distribution of psychoactive drugs is zealously monitored, penalties for abuse are stiff, and even legitimate research with drugs like LSD has dried up.

Science Sings for Its Supper

Sex, drugs, and rock 'n' roll—you're wondering how the third member of that riotous trio fits into the scientific life, aren't you. Very peripherally, is the answer; but, in my case, in close connection with something that lies at the very heart of that life—the funding of grants.

How to get research funds may in fact be the number one preoccupation of all scientific researchers. This is especially true for sleepwatchers because of the difficulty in getting anyone excited about the sleeping brain. Grants are the lifeblood of the academic physician, and getting them is highly competitive. The process includes an exquisite form of torture known as the site visit. This is when the "suits" show up—peer scientists chosen to come into your lab and judge whether your research project merits new, or continued, financial support. Since the career of the average scientist depends upon uninterrupted funding, the site visit has an undeniable life-and-death quality. When it is over, although the outcome is never absolutely certain, there is a sense of relief at having survived, joy if things went well, and glum expressions all around if the visit was disastrous or labored.

In these tense encounters, you need every edge you can get—and I've stooped to just about anything that I thought might work. On one occasion I tried evoking some "good vibes" from the distant past to work their magic spell. I happened to know that one of the site visitors, then in his 40s, had been a musician in the Druids—a high school rock band that was locally very popular 25 years earlier. Another former Druid (Bill Gonda, now a San Francisco pediatrician) was the son of Tom Gonda, a colleague of mine at the Stanford medical school; the band had played at one of our laboratory parties, and I was thus able to recall its style and artistry with some authenticity. I recounted for this visitor a memory from 1966. I was driving my family home from the Beatles' last concert in Candlestick Park in San Francisco, and we had picked up three young female concert-goers who were thumbing a ride. When I observed, tongue in cheek, that the Beatles might even be as good as the Druids, the girls had squealed, "*You* know the Druids? The Druids are even *better* than the Beatles!" Bill Gonda at that time was helping out in my lab, and the fact that I was actually then "boss" of a Druid was almost more than the girls could stand. All the way home, I basked in this vicarious adulation. As I related my story during the site visit, the former Druid's eyes glowed with pleasure and nostalgia. It cannot have harmed our cause.

I haven't always had the likes of "Druidmania" to soften up the visitors, but there are other ways to strike up a harmony. One day back in 1972, I went home at about 5 o'clock after a grueling but apparently successful site visit. In the refrigerator was a bottle of excellent champagne, ready for the celebration of precisely such a success. My wife was not home yet, but rather than sit around and wait for her to appear, I opened the bottle and poured myself a glass. It was very good, and the relief was great. Glass followed glass, and I began to think about going to bed, as I had been up at 3am that morning to make final preparations for the day's challenge.

I was quite drunk, sitting in the kitchen with what I am sure was a very glazed expression on my face, when the telephone rang. I made my way to the phone and picked it up. It was the chairman of the site-visit committee. "There are several more crucial questions we need to ask you," he said. "Could you come over to the motel and meet with us again for a little while?"

"Sure," I foolishly said, with a sinking feeling. I could barely stand up.

Just then my wife walked in, and I managed to tell her what had happened. Angel that she is, she spared me the disgrace of a lecture on the folly of drinking while sleep-deprived. She quickly brewed some coffee, I downed several cups, and she drove me to the motel. "Just tell them the truth," she said. So I did. It was all my wife's fault, I explained to the committee in that little conference room. If she had been there, I would have been able to drink only half the bottle. They laughed. The grant was funded.

Laughter is a good omen. Recently, I arrived for a site visit in our conference room with an Egg McMuffin in hand. "When I was a young investigator," I recalled, "my wife would get up early and cook me a good breakfast before a site visit. Now that I am a senior investigator, I have to go to McDonald's." The visitors laughed; another grant was funded.

I don't mean to give the impression that research funding and the advancement of science in today's world depends entirely on such vagaries, but grant applications are so competitive that I do believe good science can fail to be supported simply because a reviewer is feeling grumpy.

Drama is another effective technique. In 1967, we were hoping to renew the grant for a study of the effect of prolonged REM-sleep deprivation in cats. We had begun to see a cluster of behavioral changes accompanying this procedure. The site visitors met in a conference room and then went to visit the laboratory. As they entered the lab, they heard the horrendous scream of an angry cat. Suddenly a streak of black shot into the room, ricocheted off the walls, and disappeared out the other door. One of my lab assistants, George Mitchell, appeared holding a bleeding hand. "That cat was perfectly tame and affectionate before the REM deprivation," I murmured. Once again, we got the grant.

Fear and Loathing and the Visitors from Hell

Not all of my quests for grants have gone so well. Perhaps my greatest test occurred in the mid-1970s; the remnants of the stress from that period have continued to plague me and will likely do so for the remainder of my life.

In 1975, we were sitting on top of the world, what with our successful initiation of the sleep disorders program, coming on the heels of what we considered the great discoveries of the early 1970s—discoveries about insomnia, narcolepsy, the full clinical impact of sleep apnea syndrome, the central regulation of breathing during sleep, and the role of circadian physiology in sleep disorders. In that fateful year, we put together a very large grant proposal, because funding for a number of our projects had to be renewed if they were to continue.

As I had to be in the area for another purpose, I decided for the first time to personally deliver our 1,000-plus-page proposal, written hastily in the latter part of 1974 and early 1975, to the Division of Research Grants at NIH headquarters in Bethesda, Maryland. Accordingly, I got my first peek at the room that housed these documents. It was chilling. Grant proposals were stacked up everywhere. A seasoned investigator at the age of 46, I naively asked, "Is this the warehouse for old grants?"

"No," I was told, "these are new grants of the current cycle." My perspective underwent an instantaneous, humbling change when our great, life-or-death grant proposal was taken from my hands and tossed onto a huge pile.

Our proposal was eventually rejected by a group of judges for whom smallness was a virtue. The responsible official told someone at Stanford to give me the word so I would get cracking on new grants. Unfortunately, that communication did not come until I was in Europe, at the Second International Congress of Sleep Research in Edinburgh, feeling absolutely certain that the program would be renewed and our large staff funded. I remember vividly standing in one of those English red telephone booths, where I had placed a call to the States, when I learned the grant had been rejected. The impact was devastating. I had yet to go to these meetings, keep a stiff upper lip, and continue on to France for the First International Scientific Symposium on Narcolepsy, all the while staying in close touch with the United States to see what could be done.

I had helped to organize the symposium in France, along with two colleagues. One of them, Pierre Passouant from the Université de Montpellier, had arranged that it should take place at a Mediterranean resort, La Grande Motte. As it turned out, this resort had a casino, to which all the narcoleptologists and spouses repaired one evening for cocktails and entertainment. My wife and I sat in the booth with Prof. and Mme. Passouant.

At the front of the room, two young actors in Shakespearean garb walked out onto a small stage. "Oh, wonderful," I thought. "We are going to hear Shakespeare in French." Not quite; the actors promptly took off all their clothes, and in a kind of ballet, demonstrated a number of sexual positions while the mayor of La Grande Motte, a large, swarthy man, laughed lasciviously. It was all somewhat surreal for a man preoccupied with the fact that, upon returning to California, his first task would be to fire or lay off lots of people and face a future that looked incredibly bleak.

By the time I got home, it was too late to do anything except try to meet the October and November deadlines. I decided to split our funding requests into individual insomnia, sleep apnea, narcolepsy, and circadian rhythm grant proposals. With Mary Carskadon's help, I cranked out four separate proposals in that short period of time, threw in another on sleep in adolescence, and submitted them to the powers that be. This strategy meant I had to face four or five separate site visits by agency officials—and, for good measure, a meeting with Blue Shield, which had to be persuaded to reimburse us for clinical sleep tests. I remember them all vividly. The first, the Blue Shield meeting, was on December 5; the circadian rhythm site visit came on December 10, the narcolepsy visit on December 14, the sleep and adolescents visit on December 20, the insomnia visit on January 2—the day after New Year's, believe it or not—and the toughest, the sleep apnea visit, on January 6.

At the height of my powers, here I was, facing the possible death of my research programs and my career. We worked day and night over a four-week period, drinking pots of coffee to stay awake in order to prepare for each new onslaught. By the last visit on January 6, toward the end of the day, battered by a barrage of tough questions—How can you do this? Why do you want to do so much? Why do you think this is important?—I just couldn't answer anymore. I began to see the room through a fog.

"I must be coming down with the flu," I thought. "I'm so exhausted, and it's been such a stressful month."

When the site visit finally ended, I went home. In front of my house are six steps; I was too weak to climb them. After sitting there for a moment, I half crawled up the stairs, told my wife how dead tired I was, had a small bite to eat, and fell into bed. In the morning, I went to the hospital with the classic signs of a bleeding ulcer. At the Stanford Medical Center, a test showed the concentration of my red blood cells to be less than half its normal level. X-rays were taken.

In fact I did not have an ulcer; I had stress gastritis with erosion and bleeding. While the site visitors were examining me, grilling me, torturing me, I had been literally bleeding to death. That, ladies and gentlemen, is the grant business. But the story has a happy ending. Every grant was funded, and we entered another period of growth and productivity.

This is not to say that the anxiety over getting grants ended in 1976; it is a recurring nightmare for every sleep-watcher. In 1980, our group had submitted a proposal to do a large scale study of cardiovascular stress during sleep among older individuals. The key tool in this study was to be an ambulatory monitor developed by my colleague, Laughton Miles. A computer connected to the monitor would instantly analyze the heart rate and identify the symptoms of obstructive sleep apnea.

We decided that I would wear the monitor during the first day and night of the two-day site visit, and then download it before their eyes on the afternoon of the next day. The effect would be very dramatic. On the other hand, if it didn't work, we were dead. On the afternoon of the second day, I took off the monitor; we plugged it into the computer and displayed the results on a screen. The device worked perfectly. It showed my heart rate hitting about 150 at the beginning of the site visit when I was speaking, hovering around 120 for most of the day, going down while I was asleep that night, and coming up again the next day—a clear reflection of my body's reaction to stress. The visitors were very impressed.

Just last year, I encountered Miles at a wedding, and I recalled my anxiety over the risk we had taken. "You needn't have worried," he said, "I had loaded some dummy data into the computer, just in case we needed it. As it turned out, we didn't." A student of mine wore the same monitor at his Ph.D. oral examination sometime later on, and we found that his heart rate reached the pathological level of 157 when the questions were particularly difficult. I have always intended to write a letter to *Science* magazine about the stresses of academic life, but I've been so busy worrying about getting my grants funded that I've never found the time.

The Show Must Go On

And "If I had it all to do over again...?" Nobody egotistical enough to write a book about their work is likely to answer that they would do something else. However, I have to think twice before promising an eager young student— not unlike myself in 1951—a lifelong career in sleep research. I feel more optimistic about this than I ever have in the past, but with hundreds of conflicting priorities in spending the public dollar, there is no certainty in any field, let alone in sleep research.

I have mentioned earlier the stunning discrepancy between the large number of neuroscientists studying the waking brain and the handful who are studying the sleeping brain. This discrepancy is all the more astonishing if we postulate that the functions of the sleeping brain are as complex and numerous as the functions of the waking brain. Among the most frustrating parts of my life is hearing the frequent questions that begin, "Have you done...?" Have you studied blind people? What about Olympic athletes? Have you studied frogs? Time after time, I am forced to explain that the amount of funding for sleep research is so small, and the number of sleepwatchers so few, that it may be several centuries before we get around to studying all the things people ask about. Our only hope for satisfying a lively public curiosity—not to mention the tremendous medical need to understand sleep in all its aspects—is to increase both the number of scientists and the amount of research dollars.

In my early scientific life, I never questioned the priorities of society, the NIH, academia, or even my colleagues. I just assumed some benign and wise manager was watching out and would make sure that the right thing happened. Today, I know better; in some vitally important areas of sleep research and sleep disorders, *not one single study has been done.*

There are thousands of scientific journals now in existence throughout the world. If each includes ten to twenty research papers per issue and publishes ten issues per year, we have millions of scientific studies published annually. The number dealing with sleep is an infinitesimal segment of this amount—less than 0.001 percent. Alas, public curiosity has not been matched by a vigorous societal mandate, and those of us in the field must still struggle mightily for our research funds.

Can I see myself at the age of 90, hunched over yet another grant proposal and hobbling to the lab for another site visit? I don't know. Today, science is more exciting than ever, and our lab has financial security for a few more years. The age of mandatory retirement is currently at 70 and will soon be removed altogether. I believe that the two keys to my scientific longevity are the relative youth of the field I work in and the slowness with which it has advanced. If we look at molecular biology since it was electrified by the advent of the double helix, we see advance following upon advance with dazzling rapidity. It would be interesting to know what percentage of the scientists in that field have managed to keep going for forty years. We sleepwatchers, on the other hand, have still to establish our baselines by recording normal people all night long and then checking their alertness the next day. This could have been done fifty years ago if the effort had been made, and it could keep some of us busy for quite a while.

But enough of this morose introspection—the fact is, the scientific life has been good to me. The process of discovery is remarkably sustaining. It is also fun to organize new knowledge and tell people about it; the cycle is natural and self-restoring. As scientist Lewis Thomas, author of *Lives of a Cell*, has written, communication is the salient feature of the human condition. And indeed, scientists do a lot of communicating. We organize ourselves into groups and societies; we lecture to students and to each other. And we love it.

Part of what we love, of course, is having a large audience; but we are not always so lucky. At a place like Stanford University, there is intense competition for the attention of faculty and students. I might invite a prestigious guest to come and give a lecture, and then have only four or five people show up in a large lecture hall to listen.

Even today, I find this the single most unnerving thing that can happen in my day-to-day routine. Once I invited a doctor from Belgium to give a lecture at Stanford. To my dismay, in spite of our having flooded the campus publicity, the guest speaker and I found ourselves on the stage facing an audience of two people. It was more like a bridge game than a prestigious lecture. I was jack-knifed with embarrassment, though it was not mentioned then or ever again. Sometime thereafter, a noted professor from France was visiting Stanford and was scheduled to give a talk. Anticipating that the audience might be a little thin, I ordered everyone in my office—secretaries, typists, accountants, students—to attend the lecture.

The largest audience that I myself have ever spoken before was at the annual meeting of the American Academy of Family Physicians in Dallas, Texas, about ten years ago. The auditorium was very large, with a single door at the back. There were two keynote speakers; I was one, and Denton Cooley, the famous heart surgeon, was the other. He had just been the subject of a *Time* cover story called "The Artificial Heart," and about 5,000 doctors had come to hear what Cooley had to say about this promising new mechanism. While Cooley spoke, I sat looking around the auditorium, thrilled by the huge audience. Unfortunately, when I stood up to talk, about half the audience got up to leave. I lectured for about an hour to 2,500 physicians, while another 2,500 were struggling to get out that lone back door.

Perhaps the treacherous nature of audiences helps explain why my involvement over the years with Stanford undergraduate education has been so gratifying. It started in 1970, when, in order to keep the students indoors during one of the most disruptive and chaotic times in the University's history, I offered a course on sleep and dreams, comprised of evening lectures in the small residential lounge of the freshman dormitory where my wife and I lived for a year as faculty residents. The course was well attended and sufficiently interesting that it attracted the attention of large numbers of students outside the dorm who wanted to attend.

In order to deal with the demands of these students, who in those days were accustomed to having their demands met in some way or other, I agreed to teach the course again the very next quarter. To my simultaneous pleasure and dismay, about 450 students preregistered. Since no classroom had been reserved, there was only one place where so many students could be accommodated—the Stanford Memorial Church. And so I spent two hours, once a week, literally in the pulpit of the cavernous campus church. I had a great time pacing back and forth across the marble steps at the front of the altar, declaiming to the 600-700 students in my "congregation." The following year, the course moved to Dinkelspiel Auditorium, where I continued to enjoy audiences of some 800 students a year for the next seven years.

Here's an easy way to assure yourself an audience. Go back to your hometown under the banner "Local Boy Makes Good." That's what I did in spring of 1984—went back to Walla Walla, Washington, to participate in a symposium on sleep and to give a public lecture in the evening. For the lecture, which was sponsored by Whitman College, I was to receive an honorarium of $500. My then 94-year-old mother, who still lives in Walla Walla (as I write this, she is 101), planned to attend the lecture. I was pleased, as my parents had never quite understood what my career was all about. "Please spend all of the honorarium on publicity," I told my host. "I'd like a large turnout."

Five hundred dollars can buy a lot of publicity in Walla Walla, Washington. For a whole week there were half-page ads hawking my lecture. When the time came, my mother and I walked into the auditorium to find an overflow crowd. Some 500 people were squished into chairs, standing at the back, squatting in the aisles; a few were on the stage. As my mother looked around, I could see she was impressed that her son could attract such an audience. She sat in the front row, next to my host.

The lecture was unusually long; I had asked for at least an hour and a half, so I could say everything that needed to be said about sleep. Halfway through, my mother had to go to the bathroom. She stood up and looked frantically around; the aisles were completely blocked. She spotted a door in the front of the room next to the stage and walked over to it, but it was stuck. I had the eerie experience of talking away as my mother was rattling the auditorium door trying to get out. This seemed to go on forever, until finally my host overcame his paralysis, opened the door, and helped my mother on her errand.

I looked at the crowd and, in one of the very few episodes of lightning wit in my entire life, said, "Well, I figured somebody would walk out on me while I was talking, but I never dreamed it would be my very own mother."

Red-Eyed Roosters and Sleepwalking the Dog

Is there anything more symbolic of the line between sleeping and waking than a rooster's crow in the early morn? With that characteristic sound, the barnyard wakens—cows, horses, pigs, sheep are all roused from their nightly slumbers. Like humans, animals have daily sleep/wake cycles. And, just as in other branches of medical science, studies and experiments on animals have contributed greatly to our knowledge about the nature and patterns of human sleep.

By the early '60s, sleepwatchers had observed full-blown REM sleep in nearly the entire stable—donkeys, dogs, mice, rabbits, pigs, goats, and sheep—but not in adult birds, including chickens. Since chickens had been found to have only non-REM sleep, or 99.9 percent non-REM sleep, I was curious about how they would be affected by sleep deprivation. Bill Gonda, then a high school student (and a rocking Druid, you may recall) whose father was a professor of psychiatry at Stanford, expressed an interest in doing research with me. I suggested that he sleep-deprive chickens and see what happened.

The first experiments were done in Gonda's back yard, but around that time I obtained research facilities in a Quonset hut on the grounds of the Menlo Park Veterans Administration Hospital. We were allowed to maintain two species of experimental animals—cats and rats—by permission of the director of the center. For reasons I never did understand, we were denied permission to use chickens.

As the Quonset hut was seldom, if ever, entered by the director or anyone else on the hospital staff, we decided to risk one quick experiment, and quietly ordered four chickens. We were expecting young hens—not too large. Instead we got roosters—four gigantic roosters. They seemed to be about three feet tall, an unbelievable size. Furthermore, they still had sharp, two-inch spurs on their legs, and they were vicious; they would attack anyone who entered the room. And, as roosters are inclined to do, they crowed.

A rooster's crow is not something that can be hidden or disguised easily. When the director showed up unexpectedly one day, demanding to know what was going on, the roosters were in full voice. Everyone working in the laboratory at the time began to cough and sneeze and make other distracting noises, but to no avail. I very nearly lost both the facility and my good name. The chicken experiment was never done and remains, so far as I know, one of the loose ends of sleep research.

We've had better luck with other species. In fact, animals have been of vital importance to many of our discoveries. Our understanding of narcolepsy was greatly increased, for example, by our possession of a colony of narcoleptic dogs. In 1972, we showed a movie of a human narcoleptic patient having a cataplectic attack at the annual convention of the American Medical Association in San Francisco. A doctor from Sacramento put us in touch with a veterinarian who had a dog that seemed to do the same thing. The dog, thought to have incurable epilepsy, had been put to sleep; however, the veterinarian had first taken a movie that showed the dog starting to eat and then collapsing in exactly the same manner (a toneless heap) as our human patients.

I attached the film clip of this dog to the end of our own film and showed it at the American Academy of Neurology in Boston in 1973. A neurologist approached me afterward to report a dog in his home town of Saskatoon with attacks just like the dog in the movie. Through him we arranged for this dog, a miniature poodle named Monique, to be flown to Stanford for testing. We found that Monique, like human narcoleptics, had emotion-precipitated episodes of muscular limpness; she also had occasional sleep onset REM periods, and she appeared to be excessively sleepy.

Hoping to breed more such animals for study, we arranged to send Monique back to Saskatoon to mate with her brother. When she came into heat I called a reputable airline, saying that I had a narcoleptic dog I wanted to send to Saskatoon. I was told, "No sick dogs on airplanes." Although I tried to explain that narcolepsy wasn't really an illness, the airline wouldn't budge. At this point I would have driven to Saskatoon, but during the 1974 gasoline crisis, with huge lines at the pump, driving was out of the question. As a last-ditch effort, I thought, Why not call my congressman? I did, and spoke to one of his aides. Fifteen minutes later the phone rang; it was the president of the airline saying he would help me in any way he could. Monique flew to Saskatoon, mated, and came back. To our dismay, she did not get pregnant.

I felt that if there was one dog there must be one more. I embarked on a national tour at my own expense, lecturing at colleges of veterinary medicine and animal care centers, describing narcolepsy, and asking veterinarians to be on the lookout for other dogs. A doctor in the school of veterinary medicine at Cornell University had a dog. Veterinarians from Florida sent us dogs. In short order, we had ten or twelve dogs with narcolepsy.

A few years later, the breeding of two Dobermans resulted in a litter of seven puppies that, at the age of about eight weeks, all developed unambiguous cataplexy on virtually the same day. On December 7, 1977, this remarkable litter hit national TV. Our narcolepsy colony was established. In these animals, we have found brain abnormalities in exactly the areas that mediate REM sleep. The disease is transmitted in dogs by a recessive gene we call *canarc-1*; this gene, or one very similar to it, may also be floating around in the human population. A member of our sleep research team, Emmanuel Mignot, is now trying to isolate and characterize *canarc-1*; by the time you read this, he may have succeeded. It is possible that identifying the chromosomal site of this abnormal gene will reveal other genes that are extremely important in regulating sleep mechanisms.

Choices: Animals or Humans

The world is contradictory and paradoxical. Almost nothing in life is 100 percent good or 100 percent bad. We must make difficult choices; no matter how sound our reasons for those choices, there is inevitably a downside. Often, time must pass before "correct" choice becomes obvious. I have spent a good part of my career doing research with animals as subjects. The only rational approach to understanding the function of sleep available at present is the deprivation study, but this direction of research has been jeopardized by the animal rights movement.

Sleep research is inherently organismic. That is, we cannot sleep-deprive a single cell, or even know if there are cellular changes over time that could be considered analogous to sleep and wakefulness. Accordingly, we sleep-deprive animals. Why animals? Because long-term sleep deprivation carries a definite risk, and society permits more risk for animals than for humans.

For sleep deprivation in animals we must use implanted electrodes as opposed to scalp and skin surface electrodes, which will not stay in place—most animals will simply claw them off. With the animal under anesthesia, we make a vertical slit down the midline of the top of the head; we use retractors to carefully spread apart the skin and muscle; then we place small screws in the skull to make contact with the surface of the dura mater. Electrode wires are attached to these screws. The surface of the skull, the screws, and the wires are then covered with dental cement, forming a small skull cap. A cable can be plugged into the skull cap and attached to the monitors. This procedure appears to cause absolutely no discomfort to the animal, who seems not even to notice it.

Because most of our animal sleep-deprivation studies have had no apparent permanent effects, the "what next?" issue always arises for these animals. Through a reverse procedure, again under anesthesia, the skull cap and screws can be removed, the muscle and skin sutured at the midline; to all intents and purposes, the animal is totally restored. But finding homes for these rehabilitated research subjects has proved to be very difficult, if not impossible. On occasion we have approached individuals in the animal rights movement who have loudly expressed concern about research animals, but their concern apparently does not extend to giving rehabilitated veterans a home.

The animal rights movement would stop all sleep research on animals if it could. Patients with narcolepsy do not want this research stopped; neither do the parents of sudden infant death syndrome (SIDS) victims, nor do patients whose family members have died from fatal familial insomnia. We must choose between human beings and animals.

My daughter was run down by a speeding automobile in February of 1987, and she sustained a severe, traumatic brain injury. Today she is partially recovered, but will probably never recover completely; her chance for a normal life was destroyed. It might all have been different.

Most of the damage in traumatic brain injury is secondary to the enzymes that are released when cells break down. This causes a cascade of widespread damage whereby the breakdown of cells injures other cells, which break down and injure other cells, and so on.

As I write, new treatments are undergoing widespread clinical trials. These treatments involve injecting compounds, shortly after an injury, that prevent secondary damage. In animal experiments, which had to be done in Spain and Canada because they could not be done in the United States, it was shown that severe injury to the brain of cats could not even be detected in animals that had been treated with these compounds. Had animal rights activism—and in some cases, active terrorism—not slowed the progress of research in the '70s, this treatment would by now surely have been available for my daughter and countless other victims as well.

8

The Mysteries That Lure Us On

T he most beautiful thing we can experience is the mysterious. It is the source of all true art and science.

—Albert Einstein
"What I Believe," *Forum*, October 1930

In spite of all that has been said, in spite of all that sleepwatchers have done to date, the most fundamental questions about sleep still remain. Surely they pique the curiosity of every conscious human being. Why do we sleep? What is the function of sleep? What purpose does it serve?

We Sleep, It Seems, Because We Must

Two biological factors seem to affect and regulate sleep. One of these is the *biological clock*, which acts something like a natural internal alarm clock, sometimes telling us when to wake up and other times allowing us to go to sleep. I spoke of the functions and problems of this clock in Chapter 5. Another factor is *homeostasis,* the regulation of a function by feedback to maintain a healthy level.

There is no question that the amount of sleep is homeostatically regulated and that the drive to sleep, as I explained in Chapter 1, is increased as a result of prior reduction of the amount of sleep obtained. This is very similar to the increase in the biological drive to seek food or water based on prior deprivation. There is both a physiological state and an associated psychological feeling: with food deprivation, we feel hunger; with fluid deprivation, thirst; and with sleep deprivation or reduction, sleepiness. This may be the primary force behind the sleep drive: Less sleep is generally followed by more sleep, and more sleep by less—although the latter is harder to prove because it is difficult to induce unneeded sleep without using drugs.

Even if we can biologically explain what causes *the urge* to sleep, the most basic question still remains. What is the function of sleep? There must be some vital purpose, some insurmountable need, requiring us to sleep. I had originally thought that the answer to the riddle of sleep would come from sleep-deprivation studies. It still may, but I am beginning to feel that understanding the molecular basis of sleep may give us the answer first—or, rather, the answers. Sleep-deprivation experiments have their limitations. The drive to sleep intensifies progressively as deprivation continues, soon becoming so overwhelming that voluntary wakefulness is no longer possible. Eventually, the subject must be poked and prodded so frequently that the experiment becomes unpleasant, stressful, and potentially painful. Many researchers feel that there is no way to adequately eliminate stress from sleep-deprivation experiments.

The fact that the sleep drive is so powerful doesn't absolutely prove that sleep *per se* has any active vital function. An opposing view is that sleep may instead be an adaptive process. Gazing back down the evolutionary trail, some investigators have speculated that the function of the sleep drive, together with its biological timing, is to force the organism to seek a safe place and to create "down time" just when that organism is adaptively most unsuited to be out and about. Human beings are essentially helpless in the dark: rats and mice are easy prey in the sunlight. For safety's sake, it is better to hide at these times. This prolonged time of immobility has an additional major benefit for the organism—conserving calories. Hibernation, a possible adaptive extension of sleep, carries the conservation of calories to the ultimate extreme.

But if that's all sleep is for, then what about REM sleep? Getting into a safe place does not require a complex mechanism for cerebral activation and muscular paralysis. Then again, nature can be redundant and somewhat wasteful. The entire human gene complex, to take an example, is duplicated each time one of the body's trillions of cells divides—even tens of thousands of genes that particular type of cell will never use. A complex mechanism to get us through the night? Why not? And if it is coupled to a dream show, all the better.

Suppose that, indeed, sleep serves only an adaptive function to conserve calories, or to motivate the organism to seek a safe place. Might we not then speculate that in the modern world, where calorie conservation and safety are not issues, it may someday be possible to eliminate sleep and thus greatly extend the amount of time we can spend awake—and, by implication, our productivity? What if, however, the biological clock permits marked alertness only at certain times of the day? It certainly seems to function this way, which forces us to ask ourselves what an additional eight hours of dull, lethargic wakefulness would contribute to our existence. Not to mention that, weaned from sleep, we would lose our dreams.

There are individuals who may be very short sleepers—claiming to get as little as one to three hours of sleep per day without any apparent ill effects. Several of these claims were reported in the early 1970s, before we had invented the Multiple Sleep Latency Test to validate them; observations from those days cannot be accepted as final documentation. It is possible that some individuals have an overactive clock, which would cause a great deal of arousal and override the sleep debt. On the other hand, one would think that if sleep debt were progressively increasing as a result, the "manic" clock would at some point be challenged beyond its capacity. Recently I encountered a physician who is practicing medicine full-time and also serving as president of a thriving business and a member of the Young Presidents Organization. This busy man, whose age was about 40 and who seemed normal, claimed to sleep only one or two hours a day. Alas, he would not submit to the laboratory observation that could prove his claim.

If indeed such short sleepers exist, we would have to assume one of three things: (1) that in these individuals, the biological purpose of sleep, whatever it might be, is carried out in a relatively brief amount of time and that the homeostatic drive, normally working to adapt to a 24-hour environmental cycle, is not functioning powerfully in these cases; (2) that in such people, the putative necessary function of sleep is carried out in the waking state by some mutation; or (3) that there really, truly is no vital need for sleep. This latter possibility boggles my mind; how could it be true, given the complexity of evolving and periodically inducing totally different states in the brain, or given the intricacies of REM sleep.

Two Aspirins, a Little Chicken Soup—and Plenty of Rest

In our search for the function or functions of sleep, we must consider the possibility that it plays a role in the ability to fight disease. As far back as I can remember, the most common prescription in medicine has always been, "Go to bed. Get lots of sleep." Most sick people do indeed go to bed, but we still do not know for sure whether they really get more sleep when they are ill. It certainly seems that way, but systematic studies are virtually nonexistent.

Conversely, stress and exhaustion may foster the development of disease. Although popular belief has it that sleep deprivation increases the risk of becoming ill, I'm not so sure myself. Of the relatively few subjects we have totally sleep-deprived, none were unable to complete the experiments. For example, as I've mentioned earlier, we studied one high-school student who stayed awake for eleven days and remained healthy throughout. While it might be interesting to track the levels of various immune factors in the blood over the course of a sleep-deprivation experiment, using today's ultra-precise methodology, ethical concerns are such that these experiments are ever more unlikely to be run.

It is very difficult to find any distinction between sleeping and waking as they relate to the immune response, which is carried out primarily by white blood cells. We fight disease on a continual 24-hour basis; bacteria enter our bodies all the time. There is thus no reason to assume that white blood cells would participate in the daily cycle of sleep and wakefulness.

But we might be entirely wrong. It is possible to speculate that the period of sleep is used in some way to fine-tune the immune system, or to do something with the immune system that cannot be done as easily during wakefulness. There are a number of tantalizing findings. If we observe human beings around the clock, we see during sleep a peak in the blood levels of immune-response regulators called interleukens. One speculation, which has not been confirmed, is that high levels of interleukens in the blood actually are responsible for fostering the occurrence of sleep. In fact, nearly all the immune-response factors in the blood are potent sleep inducers. This fact may account for the sleepiness that appears to be present during the acute onset of an infectious disease.

Years ago, having become skillful at wiring myself with electrodes using a mirror, I would often, after a night of monitoring a subject, hook myself up to the polygraph machine. I was thus able to gather a great deal of data on my own sleep. One afternoon I became ill with what appeared to be viral influenza. By the time evening approached, I felt awful and had a mild fever. I hooked myself up, went to bed, and spent a night that seemed very restless, even somewhat hallucinatory. At any rate, in the morning I had recorded about eight to ten hours of sleep, with *no REM sleep whatsoever*. This is the sum total of my own experience with sleep and febrile illness. What can it mean? What's the significance? I don't know.

I Am Curious—Pillowtalk

We must also ask, Why are there two kinds of sleep? The implication is that there may be two entirely different main functions, one attached to REM and one to non-REM sleep. Which is the primary state? Since REM sleep is present in mammals and birds (just barely) but apparently not in reptiles, most speculation has related it to functions of the higher organisms. In this remarkable state, the brain shuts off the motor neurons in the spinal cord and then, if brain waves are any indication, goes into a tremendously accelerated existence in which it creates another world and, in its giving structure to consciousness, "lives" in that world. Is this consciousness necessary? Or are consciousness and self-awareness merely an ineluctable by-product of the activity of the evolutionarily advanced brain? This does not appear to be the case in non-REM sleep.

The questions go on and on. That sheer curiosity has not impelled countless numbers of scientists to pursue these mysteries, I find difficult to understand. Does the dream itself serve a necessary purpose, or even an unnecessary purpose? Why is there so much REM sleep in infancy? Do babies dream? I have already (in Chapter 2) detailed my theory, developed with Howard Roffwarg, that REM sleep is related to the development of the nervous system. The theory has yet to be proven. Could we someday control REM sleep and live in the dream world? (This would be akin to lucid dreaming.) If we knew enough about sleep, could we eliminate it? Or could we eliminate the homeostat so that we would never get sleepy and would merely induce sleep at our whim so that it could then carry out its biological purposes?

Decades of sleep-deprivation experiments have failed to yield convincing answers to any of these questions. In recent years, as discussed in Chapter 3, Allan Rechtschaffen and his colleagues have shown that selective REM deprivation is fatal in rodents. Rechtschaffen's current attempt to document the various disturbances that lead to death may at some point allow us to infer and test the vital and not-so-vital functions of sleep. Meanwhile, my hope is that as the molecular understanding of sleep mechanisms proceeds, we will stumble upon some physiological, biochemical, or genetic oddity that will reveal the secret of sleep and allow us to bypass stressful sleep-deprivation methodologies, explain past results, and enable scientists to design more effective experiments in the future.

We must always keep in mind that the sleeping brain may do quite a number of things. Some of these may be relatively trivial and perhaps mainly for our entertainment while we are asleep. Certainly we devote a lot of energy to entertaining ourselves when we are awake; why not also during the other third of our lives? In any case, the potential of the sleeping brain and the sleeping mind may be enormously greater than we now realize. I have speculated in Chapter 6 that the true function of the dream is for future, as yet unrevealed, purposes of humanity.

Pleasant Dreams

Just because I stay up all night thinking about these things doesn't mean you have to. I'd hate to be responsible for yet another case of insomnia. If this has been your bedtime reading, it's time to put the book down, release one muscle group at a time, breathe deeply and slowly ...relax...and let the active sleep processes take over and carry out their nocturnal tasks. Good night.

9

Update 1995

There have been some important developments in the world of sleep since *The Sleepwatchers* was marketed by the Stanford University Alumni Association early in 1992. It would seem both unfair and counterproductive to reissue *The Sleepwatchers* without describing at least those developments that everyone should know about.

In order to accomplish this, I have chosen simply to add an "Update 1995." The following are not *all* the advances which one sleepwatcher or another would deem important, but mainly my personal choice of those which I feel should be part of our national sleep awareness agenda. In addition, leaving the original text unchanged will allow the reader to gain a clear picture of how rapid progress has been in several areas over the course of the intervening four years.

Obstructive Sleep Apnea: Highly Prevalent and Potentially Lethal

We now know for certain that obstructive sleep apnea is sufficiently common and sufficiently dangerous that everyone should be aware of it. In 1993, a group led by the distinguished epidemiologist, Terry Young, working in the sleep disorders center at the University of Wisconsin published their findings on population prevalence. They found that 24 percent of adult males and 9 percent of adult females had obstructive sleep apnea. This extrapolates to 30 million Americans, a truly gigantic number. This number includes all victims from the mildest to the most severe. About a third, or 10 million Americans have a moderate to severe level of obstructive sleep apnea and should be considered for treatment. A somewhat smaller number were found to have symptoms of excessive sleepiness. However, I now believe that the sleepiness associated with obstructive sleep apnea is drastically underreported. Quite frankly, loud snoring alone is enough to establish a high index of suspicion.

The prevalence tends to increase with age. Several studies show that 10 to 30 percent of all individuals over 65 have obstructive sleep apnea. The tendency for males to outnumber females decreases as we age. In view of the gigantic prevalence of obstructive sleep apnea, I say again, it is important that *everyone* have some sort of sleep and breathing evaluation in their adult life.

Two current treatments for obstructive sleep apnea were both introduced in 1981. The reversal of obstructive sleep apnea by continuous positive airway pressure

(CPAP) applied through the nostrils was first reported by the Australian pulmonologist, Colin Sullivan and his colleagues in 1981. The treatment of obstructive sleep apnea by the surgical procedure, uvulopalatopharyngoplasty (UPPP), was reported by the late Shiro Fujita and his colleagues also in 1981. In subsequent years, UPPP, which had great initial popularity because it appeared to eliminate the need for chronic tracheostomy, has not been as effective as was initially hoped. However (see below), it has given way to more sophisticated and effective surgical procedures.

Nasal CPAP acts predominantly by providing a physical "pressure" splint to the upper airway. This prevents the inspiratory suction from collapsing the airway. The treatment is very effective. However, the long term use of nasal CPAP (all night every night) requires considerable understanding and commitment by the patient. Some women will develop obstructive sleep apnea during pregnancy. They snore and they gain weight. What is the effect on the developing fetus? Any woman who has been diagnosed with sleep apnea before or during pregnancy must be treated. Obviously, if the oxygen level decreases markedly during sleep, it will impact the developing fetus.

Surgical treatment is indicated for patients who cannot tolerate nasal CPAP. Successful surgical treatment of obstructive sleep apnea can only be documented conclusively by a follow-up sleep study. When this is done following UPPP, relatively few obstructive sleep apnea patients have a satisfactory result. In recent years, Nelson Powell and Robert Riley, surgeons working with the Stanford Sleep Clinic, in well over 500 cases, have successfully treated patients utilizing a combination of ENT and maxillofacial procedures. The most commonly used approach to achieve maximum favorable results while at the same time limiting hospitalizations and surgical costs is a procedure combining UPPP and a limited anterior sagittal osteotomy with genioglossus advancement and hyoid suspension.

Finally, a variety of dental appliances have been developed for the treatment of obstructive sleep apnea. At the present time, such approaches should be viewed with skepticism because follow-up data objectively documenting successful treatment are very sparse, and extensive evaluation of compliance has not been done.

When there is a high likelihood that someone has obstructive sleep apnea, they should be referred to a sleep disorders center, where the patient can receive a thorough explanation of the problem and the serious consequences if the disease is ignored. Once diagnosed and treated, the most common outcome is that an individual will be living with nocturnal CPAP for the foreseeable future.

There is some debate whether five to ten obstructive events per hour has any clinical significance. The Wisconsin group found that about one third had 15 or more events. In my opinion, the best way to characterize the prevalence of this sleep disorder is to state that 20 million Americans are in the early stages of obstructive sleep apnea, and 10 million need treatment. Of the latter, treatment is an emergency for about 5 million. Therefore, today we are justified in stating that the most serious and costly illness in America, in terms of outcome if untreated and the total number of victims, is obstructive sleep apnea. It is a moral imperative that every primary care physician recognize this problem in their patients and treat it when necessary. When the illness is severe, treatment is typically experienced as a miracle of restoration. To the extent that this incredible benefit is blocked by medical insurance policy guidelines, 30 million victims and their families working together can change any situation if they become educated and empowered.

Restless Legs Syndrome:
A Correction and an Apology

The first edition of *The Sleepwatchers* was not a scholarly work. In fact, I dictated it in less than a month and relied almost entirely on my experience and my memory. By some quirk of fate, during the time when I was working every day in our sleep disorders clinic, I saw very very few patients with Restless Legs Syndrome. Though it was described in the scientific literature, there was no prevalence study, and I stated, "Although fairly rare, all patients with restless legs syndrome have periodic limb movements."

Both parts of this statement have proved to be inaccurate. Though the association of periodic limb movement during sleep with restless legs syndrome is very high, it is not 100%. And, I was taken to task by Pickett Guthrie and Virginia Wilson of the Restless Legs Syndrome Foundation for the rarity statement. In their activist role in identifying victims, they have found that it is definitely not rare. In addition, doctors with a special interest in this problem were finding a high prevalence in patients' relatives.

At the present time, the Restless Legs Syndrome Foundation estimates that 12 million Americans have this problem. Very soon, the Gallup Poll Organization will do a national survey to establish the population prevalence. Unlike many sleep disorders (including obstructive sleep apnea) which require special sleep studies in order to be diagnosed, Restless Legs Syndrome can be established from an interview or questionnaire. This will be very important, because, if recognized, Restless Legs Syndrome is treatable. When severe, it is horrible because patients must walk nearly all night to experience relief from the symptoms and, for this reason, have very severe insomnia.

More Thoughts on Sleep Indebtedness

Every hour of sleep that an individual obtains less than his or her needed amount is carefully registered by the brain as a debt, and this debt is precisely tabulated over time. It is quite possible that the debt includes an hour lost a month ago or a week ago as well as last night. Obviously, this assumes that there is a specific amount of nightly sleep for each individual which will maintain the same degree of daytime physiological alertness over time. It also assumes that this amount varies somewhat from individual to individual.

For an individual who needs nine hours a night, and who sleeps six hours a night for a week, the lost sleep would add up to a debt of 21 hours by the end of the week. In other words, the human sleep debt accumulates just like a credit card balance. The brain apparently keeps very accurate figures on the sleep deficit it accrues. This sleep debt drives the tendency of the brain to fall asleep, and the amount of the debt, *not* the feeling of sleepiness, determines the level of risk that any person operating hazardous equipment or making crucial decisions may make a disastrous error. Persons who are very sleepy in the daytime, even though they are sleeping around eight hours at night and do not have a specific sleep disorder, can reduce the problem by increasing their daily amount of sleep. This is usually done by increasing the time in bed.

More Scientific Documentation of the Sleep Debt

Two similar experiments done more than two decades apart dramatically confirm the concept that human beings can unknowingly carry a large sleep debt. Neither experiment was designed by the researchers primarily to study sleep. In both experiments, brain waves were recorded continuously as one of many measurements of the effects of the experimental protocol on the human volunteers.

The first experiment was carried out more than twenty years ago at the United States Naval Hospital in Bethesda, Maryland, as a test of sensory deprivation. At that time, it was hypothesized that a substantial reduction of sensory input would dramatically impair normal mental processes, and that disorientation, hallucinations, and even psychosis might be the consequence. Subjects were required to remain in a cubicle where they were completely isolated from light, sound, and interactions with the outside world. The temperature was held constant, neither perceptibly cool nor perceptibly warm, and the subjects wore thick gloves to minimize tactile sensations. Brain waves were recorded continuously 24 hours a day by means of very thin wires that were looped through the subjects' scalps so they did not have to be replaced. Subjects remained in this sensory deprivation situation for one week.

Having absolutely nothing to do, subjects generally slept a great deal throughout the first 24-hour period. The mean total sleep time for the group was above 16 hours on the first day. However, the mean total sleep time declined on each successive day, and on the last (seventh) 24-hour period, the group mean was close to eight hours.

This experiment might be viewed as a test of the old theory that sensory bombardment of the brain was necessary to maintain wakefulness. If so, it would be an extremely negative result, because with a tremendous reduction in sensory input, sleep time did not remain high. The subjects in this experiment were young naval personnel. Since we now believe that nearly all young people are chronically sleep-deprived, it may be assumed that even if the subjects had maintained reasonably normal schedules prior to the experiment, they would have begun the sensory deprivation protocol carrying a substantial sleep debt. We may assume that this sleep debt powered an enormous increase in total sleep time when there was essentially nothing else to do all day long. However, as the sleep debt was progressively reduced, the sleep drive progressively weakened and the daily amount of sleep decreased accordingly. Even with nothing else to do all day long, the subjects were unable to sleep more than eight hours.

The second experiment, recently carried out by Thomas Wehr and his colleagues at the National Institutes of Health, examined the effect of different photoperiods (duration of time spent in the light) on human mood and function. The experiment was carried out in a laboratory setting with continuous recording of sleep parameters while subjects were in bed in the dark. When they were out of bed in the light, they were continuously observed to make sure that no sleep occurred. Each subject lived in the laboratory 24 hours a day, seven days a week, for five consecutive weeks. It should be pointed out that this type of human experimentation is very labor intensive and costs a great deal of money.

During the first seven days, the photoperiod during which subjects were out of bed in the light was the conventional 16 hours, and each day they spent the same eight hours in bed in the dark. After one week, the photoperiod was changed to ten hours, during which the subjects were out of bed in the light; and they were consequently in bed, in the dark, for 14 hours each day over the course of 28 consecutive days. During the five week period, the subjects were administered daily mood scales and a variety of other tests.

During the first week, or baseline period, the mean nightly sleep time for the subjects was 7.6 hours. This means they were awake only 24 minutes during the eight hours in bed in the dark. Assuming a sleep latency of around ten minutes, and several awakenings during the sleep period, this is a high sleep efficiency for the subjects. When the subjects were switched to the ten hour photoperiod followed by 14 hours in bed in the dark, their total sleep times jumped to daily amounts above 12 hours on the first day and then gradually declined. In the fourth week of the ten hour photoperiod schedule, total sleep time for the group had leveled off to about eight hours and fifteen minutes each day even though the opportunity to sleep remained at 14 hours.

The interpretation of these results is that the subjects entered the protocol carrying large individual sleep debts. Of course, neither the subjects nor the researchers were aware of such a possibility. The baseline period certainly did little to reduce the subjects' sleep debts and may even have resulted in a small increase. When the opportunity to sleep was greatly increased, the large sleep debt, in the same manner as in the first experiment, powered a very large increase in total daily sleep time. As the sleep debt decreased, total sleep time per day declined proportionally. If we assume that the "steady state" value in the last week of the ten hour photoperiod represented the actual daily sleep need for this group of subjects, we may conclude that all daily amounts above these values represented "extra" or "make-up" sleep. Accordingly, the mean reduction of the sleep debt averaged about thirty hours. If subjects were not at all sleep deprived, they would have to spend more than three consecutive days with no sleep at all to accumulate a sleep debt of similar magnitude. Another very notable result of this experiment was the dramatic improvement in the subjects' mood, sense of well being, and energy level as indicated by the various tests.

These experiments demonstrated that individuals who are getting what society would deem to be normal amounts of sleep, can, at the same time, be carrying a large accumulated sleep indebtedness. How long such an indebtedness would persist if no extra sleep were obtained is not known. However, it is obvious from the second experiment that to be able to sleep 30 extra hours, and to have accumulated such a debt in small increments means that sleep indebtedness must persist for substantial amounts of time—weeks or months at the very least. In addition, this experiment, and others like it, present evidence that a large sleep debt impairs our mood, our sense of well being, our energy, and our intellectual function. This means that the negative consequences of chronic sleep deprivation are not confined to having microsleeps at critical moments. There is also a general and unrecognized global impairment. Finally, it is reasonable to hypothesize that a major improvement in our function could be achieved by reducing our sleep indebtedness to a very low level. At this time, obtaining the amount of sleep we need each night should be accompanied by optimal alertness and energy each day.

The National Sleep Debt is
More Dangerous than the Monetary Debt

All we hear about today is balancing the budget and cutting all sorts of government programs. However, in my opinion, it is the *National Sleep Debt* that we should be worried about, and the newly-elected Republican Congress should have an equal fervor for doing something about this problem. In 1994, there was a dramatic footnote to "America's largest oil spill" as a consequence of the accidental grounding of the giant tanker, *Exxon Valdez*. In civil trial, the jury awarded the plaintiffs 5 billion dollars in damages. Thus, a single sleepy person cost his company in excess of 7 billion dollars (including clean-up costs), together with an untold loss of goodwill. And companies still have not taken this problem seriously on a large scale.

The pervasiveness of sleep deprivation is even more clear today than it was during the 1990-91 study of the National Commission on Sleep Disorders Research. The National Sleep Foundation, a charitable organization founded by the American Sleep Disorders Association while I was president, has taken on traffic safety as its major mission and is launching a national campaign called "Drive Alert. Arrive Alive." to bring the issue of drowsy drivers onto the front burner. It is almost certain that traffic accidents caused by falling asleep at the wheel are vastly underreported. Many states do not even have a category for "fatigue" as a cause of an accident. Accordingly, we have the grotesque situation in which there is no official cause of death when people fall asleep at the wheel.

An accident occurred recently, practically in my back yard, which dramatically emphasized the inadequacy of investigation and reporting. A two lane highway runs by my house. It is straight for a long distance and then there is a gentle curve. Recently, a car, traveling approximately 50-60 m.p.h. according to witnesses, approached the curve and without braking or changing direction drove straight into a tree. Hearing the ambulance and police car so nearby, I ran to the scene to see what had happened. The driver was dead and he was subsequently found to be free of drugs or alcohol. He looked to be about 30 years old making a heart attack highly unlikely. I asked the investigating officer if he was going to try to find out how long the victim had been driving prior to the accident, or perhaps ask a family member about his schedule during the previous week, and whether he was a loud snorer. At a certain point, the investigating officer became irritated with me and asked me to leave him alone while at the same time suggestively patting his handcuffs. The next day in the paper, he was quoted as saying, "The car had veered off the road and the cause of the accident was unknown." This is actually exactly the type of accident where the National Transportation Safety Board would follow up with an investigation of the victim's schedule, and, if appropriate, would identify fatigue as the cause.

Patient Support Groups

The National Commission on Sleep Disorders Research reported that 40 million Americans were chronically ill with sleep disorders, and untold millions suffered intermittently. The new prevalence data on obstructive sleep apnea require this total to be revised upward to 50 million chronically ill. The fact that many of the worst problems can be effectively treated and are still mainly unrecognized by doctors, is an abomination.

I have come to realize with great certainty that grass-roots advocacy and sleep disorders patient activists have the power to solve this problem. In 1988, Lucy Seger, a respiratory therapist and polysomnographic technician working with Mark Sanders in Pittsburgh established the first support group for obstructive sleep apnea patients. The patients were more helpful to one another in terms of adjusting masks, for instance, than doctors could ever be. They called themselves AWAKE. The acronym stands for Alive, Well, And Keeping Energetic! They exchanged information, experiences, tips on living with nasal CPAP and hosted speakers from the sleep research and sleep disorders community. The idea spread rapidly and the organization now has a network of over 200 groups and a newsletter. Every patient who is diagnosed should be made aware of the nearest AWAKE group. More recently, the Restless Legs Syndrome Foundation has begun to encourage the formation of local support groups for patients afflicted with this sleep disorder. This initiative also appears to be headed for great success.

In addition to responding to the needs of patients, the AWAKE Network exists to increase community awareness, to foster good insurance reimbursement policies, and in the recent past, to exert some political pressure for the implementation of the recommendations of the National Commission on Sleep Disorders Research. A new agency, the

National Center on Sleep Disorders Research, now exists in the National Institutes of Health partially as a result of the AWAKE Network's grass roots advocacy.

Within these groups are individuals who are natural born activists. In the fall of 1993, I realized that these groups could provide much needed grass roots advocacy for sleep disorders, and I began to work with them. The need to have some identity and a degree of separation led to the creation of a grass roots advocacy campaign that we now call "The Coalition to Wake Up America!" The Coalition is working to organize sleep specialists, patients, accident victims, concerned family members, and everyone we can to become visible and active in every congressional district. Our purpose is to educate the Congress, compelling them to do something about the carnage due to falling asleep in the transportation arena, nodding off on the job in all workplace situations, funding for sleep research, and bringing education about sleep onto the front burner in every component of our educational system— especially medical school education. There are 70,000 victims of obstructive sleep apnea in every congressional district. If the prevalence of Restless Legs Syndrome turns out to be equal or greater than the current estimate, there would be an additional 25,000, plus everyone with parasomnias and other sleep disorders. The total is easily *150,000 sleep disorders victims in every congressional district*. This is more people than usually vote in a congressional election and more than twice the number that usually carry the election. If all of the victims of sleep disorders were aware and active, we could rule the world.

But putting world domination aside, patient support groups can provide excellent follow-up and can foster favorable outcomes in complying with treatment. Every sleep disorders center should encourage their formation and foster their function.

More Common Sense About Sleeping Pills

There has never been a true national survey of how ordinary physicians deal with sleep disorders, and there is very little documentation about how physicians treat transient insomnia. Nonetheless, national surveys suggest that many people use sleeping pills when needed for the treatment of stress related insomnia and symptoms of jet lag. It must be assumed that much of this is relatively casual, a phone call to one's physician and a telephone prescription to the pharmacy from the physician. Probably the most common situation where physicians treat transient insomnia is in the hospital. Everyone knows it is very difficult to sleep in the hospital. Lying awake at night when one is ill, or with postoperative discomfort, is very unpleasant. When doctors are convinced that a particular sleeping pill is safe and effective, more often than not, it will be prescribed while the patient is in the hospital.

Recently, a safe and effective non-benzodiazepine sleeping pill has reached the market. The generic name is zolpidem and the trade name is Ambien. This compound is the most meticulously and extensively tested in the history of sleeping pills. Indeed, by the time Ambien was being evaluated in the 1980s, FDA clinical trials (with the advice of sleep researchers with extensive expertise in sleep pharmacology) had become scientifically elegant and sophisticated, and, for the first time, the trials replicated the recommended patterns of use in clinical practice.

Ambien goes to work rapidly and rarely, if ever, shows a daytime carryover. It is, therefore, extremely helpful in treating transient insomnia. The duration of transient insomnia can range from several nights to three weeks of disturbed sleep. The three major causes of transient insomnia are: (1) hyperarousal at night produced by excitement, anxiety, stress, anger, and/or pain; (2) circadian/biological rhythm problems, such as jet lag or abrupt schedule changes; and (3) environmental disturbances including excessive noise, extremes of temperature, or an unfamiliar sleeping environment. Transient insomnia is often called situational insomnia.

If you, the reader, have abrupt severe insomnia due to one of these causes, you are responding to reduced sleep in a normal fashion by building up a huge sleep debt and putting yourself and everyone else in danger. It is just as wrong to ignore severe insomnia as any other health problem. When the causative factor, for example environmental stress, is removed, normal sleep will return. What I tell doctors is that if someone actually comes to them asking for something to help them sleep, and the cause is clearly one of those mentioned above, the patient is, by definition, desperate, and urgently requires treatment. Nobody goes to see a doctor because of one bad night.

Unfortunately, many people, including doctors, feel that insomnia is not a real problem and that treating insomnia with sleeping pills is akin to swatting a mosquito with a sledge hammer. People who say this are, of course, people who have never had severe insomnia. The fact is that insomnia can be very serious. The consequences that make transient insomnia serious and dangerous are the associated daytime sleepiness and fatigue. Severe sleep loss due to transient insomnia in otherwise normal sleepers always leads to tiredness, fatigue, drowsiness, and impaired performance in the daytime. This, in turn, interferes with work and other activities, and creates a danger due to inattention or falling asleep while driving or drowsiness in some other hazardous situation. Most people refer to the increased sleep tendency as exhaustion, fatigue, tiredness, misery, but rarely as excessive sleepiness. In addition, the increasing likelihood for an inappropriate sleep episode to occur is camouflaged by the ongoing stress and anxiety.

If doctors have in the past been guilty of overusing sleeping pills, it seems clear that at the present time there is a tendency to err on the side of being overly cautious. The following vignettes excerpted from testimony presented to the National Commission on Sleep Disorders Research illustrate this point:

Carolyn G. was vacationing on the South Carolina coast with her three children, husband, sister, and brother-in-law. Her brother-in-law had a heart attack and was airlifted to a Charleston hospital. Carolyn G.'s sister departed to be at her husband's bedside leaving two small children in Carolyn G.'s care. Two days later, Iraq invaded Kuwait. Carolyn G.'s husband, a reservist, was immediately put on active duty in the Persian Gulf.

She began to experience severe insomnia as a result of anxiety about her husband and the stress of being alone with her own three children as well as her sister's two. After three nearly sleepless nights and extreme daytime exhaustion, she consulted a local physician and requested something to help her sleep. The physician refused to prescribe, saying, "Sleeping pills are addicting" and recommended hot baths at bedtime.

After the fourth night of severe insomnia, Carolyn G. decided to terminate the "vacation" and return to her home in Columbia where her mother, living nearby, could help care for the children. On the drive, she fell asleep at the wheel. Drifting into the oncoming lane, Carolyn G. and the five children miraculously escaped fatal injury in a head-on collision with a large truck.

Roger M. was a hard working young businessman. He was, as far as he knew, happily married. Upon returning from a business trip, he expected to be met at the airport by his wife. Instead, a complete stranger served him with divorce papers and gave him the keys to his car. When he arrived at his home, his wife was nowhere to be found and a number of his prized possessions were also gone. He called various acquaintances, but was unable to locate his wife.

That night, he could not sleep at all, and the following day he was extremely upset and could not work. His agitation increased as repeated attempts to locate his wife met with failure. Again, he was completely unable to sleep. After the third night of no sleep and feelings of severe anxiety and depression, he began to question his own worth and began to feel that life was not worth living. Although he was exhausted, he did not feel sleepy.

At the urging of friends, he consulted a physician for the purpose of obtaining sleep medication. The physician refused to prescribe medication and suggested he see a psychiatrist. The earliest appointment the patient could obtain was for the following week.

After five nights and days of no sleep at all, Roger M. experienced a somnambulistic amnesic episode which began in the afternoon and ended in the late evening when he "came to" and found himself standing in the bedroom of his burning house holding a loaded rifle. His shoes were on fire. He ran from the house and put the gun to his head. Fortunately, firefighters were able to grab the rifle. He was then hospitalized for treatment of his burns. In the hospital, sleep was induced with an effective hypnotic, and after several nights of good sleep, his agitation and sleeplessness disappeared and he was able to cope with his problems, which now included criminal charges of arson and attempted suicide.

Carolyn G. and Roger M. are exceptions in that they actually consulted physicians. Usually, concern about a possible moral taint associated with the use of sleeping pills prevents people from requesting medication. The above two individuals desperately needed "something to help them sleep," and should have received it.

The positive risk/benefit ratio for the proper use of sleeping pills has been well demonstrated by scientific studies. When large numbers of treated and untreated insomniacs are compared, the untreated group has many more problems, including a significantly higher occurrence of auto accidents. Such things as fatigue, poor memory, irritability, difficulty concentrating, and days lost from work are much higher in the untreated group. Underlying these problems is the simple fact that lack of sleep gives rise to serious and often dangerous daytime impairment.

The National Commission on Sleep Disorders Research

When I was writing *The Sleepwatchers*, mainly in the summer of 1991, the National Commission on Sleep Disorders Research was in the process of wrapping up its public hearings with sessions in Cleveland and Chicago. The original chartered life of this National Commission was 18 months, which made the formal termination date September 28th. Because it had become clear to me very early in the Commission's life that 18 months was not enough time to complete the tasks assigned to it by the Congress, I persuaded Senator Ted Kennedy's office to add an amendment to the 1991 NIH Reauthorization Bill which would extend the Commission's life by an additional six months. The daunting task of writing the final report was still ahead of us.

Sometime in September, I learned that the NIH Reauthorization Bill was in trouble because it rescinded the ban on human fetal tissue research. Two weeks of frantic lobbying were unsuccessful and the National Commission on Sleep Disorders Research ceased to exist on September 28, 1991 with its work undone. Once again, I faced a huge challenge without an official mandate. There was actually one last Commission meeting later in the fall to figure out what should be done. The National Institutes of Health had supplied a part time writer but her preliminary draft had not been completed.

As 1991 ended, I decided that I would have to write at least Volume I of the final report by myself. Volume II would be a collection of scientific reviews, some of which had already been written by the chairs of subcommittees. Volume I, which would be submitted to the Congress would have to be written in an entirely different style. I had spent considerable time soliciting advice from members of Congress and their staffs to determine what everyone thought would be the most effective format for a report. As it happened, my wife and daughter were away for over a month in February and March visiting my other daughter and grandchild. A Stanford graduate, Molly Haselhorst, as my number one special assistant for the National Commission, had organized all the public hearings and working meetings, read all the testimony and position papers, and knew more about the work of the Commission than perhaps any other single individual. We secured the participation of James Walsh, at the time president of the American Sleep Disorders Association, an outstanding sleepwatcher, and the person who had done more to support the work of the National Commission perhaps than anyone else in America, and his assistant, Christen Engelhardt.

Molly and I started spewing out text. Our circadian rhythms were highly complimentary. I would get up at 4-5am and immediately start dictating or doing whatever my task for the day was, and hit the sack at 8 or 9pm. Molly would appear in the early afternoon and work until 4am, leaving me her day's (night's) writing and edits. There was enough overlap in our wake time to discuss and fight over content and editorial decisions. It was very intense. We would also fax material back and forth to Jim and Christen who were working in St. Louis. In the course of about two months, we completed the final report to our satisfaction.

Before the report could go to press and be presented to Congress, we felt it was necessary to circulate our draft among the ex-Commissioners for their comments and approval. Most of the Commissioners were scientists and fairly schooled in producing scientific articles. As I said to them, dozens of times, politics and science are very different. Nonetheless, the initial response to our draft was so negative, we hardly knew what to do. In addition, the harshest critic of the document sent his letter to all the other members which pushed them even further in a negative direction and, at best, created great ambivalence. However, I stuck by my guns and finally persuaded the Commissioners that the non-scientific style was right and might even be read by key congressional staff.

To make a long story short, the report was submitted to the Congress through the NIH at the end of September 1992. Two weeks later, I received a letter from the Honorable Mark Hatfield, Senior Senator from the State of Oregon, inviting me to a special field hearing of the Senate Appropriations Committee in Portland, Oregon to consider the Commission's recommendations. I have no idea how things moved so quickly, but it is surely a world's record for this sort of thing.

Major Findings and Conclusions of the National Commission

- **Millions of Americans Are Affected by Sleep Disorders**
  During the three years that have elapsed since the National Commission completed its study and submitted its recommendations to the Congress of the United States, additional knowledge has accumulated. **We can now state with confidence that the total number of Americans affected with one or more of the 82 specific, diagnosable sleep disorders exceeds 100 million**. Some are highly prevalent; some are rare. Some are serious, even lethal; some are merely troublesome. Effective treatments are readily available and can save lives and restore victims to good health.

- **Sleep Disorders Affect All Age Groups**
  From Sudden Infant Death Syndrome in the early months of life to REM Behavior Disorders in the aged, no age is immune. Parasomnias are commonplace in growing children. Narcolepsy and Delayed Sleep Phase Syndrome strike the adolescent. Almost all sleep disorders increase in prevalence as we grow older.

- **America Is Seriously Sleep Deprived with
  Disastrous Consequences**
  Since the National Commission alerted American society, many additional observations have been made. The National Transportation Safety Board has led the way in showing that chronic sleep deprivation is the leading cause of fatal and non-fatal heavy truck accidents. Major disasters, such as the Exxon Valdez grounding, in all modes of transportation have been caused by falling asleep at the controls. The majority of young and older adults are sleep deprived and at high risk for falling asleep at the wheel.
- **There is a Pervasive Failure of Education
  About All Aspects of Sleep**
  In 1995, the facts about the nature of sleep, sleep deprivation, and sleep disorders are still not effectively presented in any educational component of American society.
- **We Pay a High Cost in Dollars, Lives, and
  Human Suffering**
  Although greatly hampered by lack of adequate databases, the National Commission was able to make estimates of the direct and indirect costs of sleep deprivation and undiagnosed and untreated or misdiagnosed and mistreated sleep disorders to American society. Given more recent information, the toll in dollars exceeds 100 billion. The toll in human suffering, devastation, death and disability defies description. It is all the more abominable because a great deal is entirely unnecessary.

Key Recommendations of the
National Commission on Sleep Disorders Research
to the Congress of the United States

It is imperative that policy makers clearly understand both the magnitude of the problems and the strategy behind the recommendations that will provide solutions. Most Americans are not fully aware of the magnitude and seriousness of the major sleep disorders such as sleep apnea, narcolepsy, the insomnias and sudden infant death syndrome. A relationship between sleep deprivation and accidents has been recognized, but few managers or workers understand the natural cycle of sleepiness and alertness, how lost sleep accumulates progressively, or how to reduce sleep-related accidents and errors. Based on these findings, it is imperative that a strong national commitment be directed to sleep and sleep disorders.

The National Commission on Sleep Disorders Research has proposed several key recommendations for immediate implementation that will ensure the greatest benefit at the smallest cost. Even if resources were unlimited, the ambitious goal of changing the way society deals with sleep could not be accomplished overnight. These key recommendations will launch a long-range national plan to create an environment in which research findings and education programs will lead to early diagnosis and prevention of sleep disorders, and reduce the impact of sleep deprivation.

• Establish a National Center

Our nation needs an accountable structure to coordinate education and research on sleep and sleep disorders. There are excellent, growing programs of sleep research in several of the NIH Institutes. However, coordinated management and accountability are necessary to ensure that the findings of basic and clinical research are applied widely for the benefit of all our citizens, and that serious gaps in research are continually identified and effectively addressed.

Each of the problems identified by the Commission had, as its root cause, the absence of specific accountability for the resolution of the problems. The Commission believes that *greater public, scientific, policy-making, clinical, and administrative attention must be focused on the study of sleep disorders and their effects on society, and cost effective, preventive solutions must be found.*

Accordingly, the Commission recommends to the Congress of the United States the simple, but inestimably important, initial step of the creation of a national focus for sleep research. It recommends the creation of a Federal entity whose mission is (a) to foster the scientific understanding of sleep and sleep disorders, (b) to translate sleep-related knowledge into the improvement of health and productivity throughout our society, (c) to provide leadership, focus, and coordination in devising and implementing an effective education campaign aimed at all health professionals, industry, policy makers, and the general public, (d) to provide guidelines and blueprints to increase research and clinical manpower, (e) to support and cooperate with other Institutes in meeting these needs, and (f) to harness the best scientific and clinical expertise to continually update the research agenda and the national plan.

Before arriving at its decision, the Commission carefully examined the model of a national center housed *within* an existing institute. There are several, but it particularly examined the relatively new National Center for Medical Rehabilitation Research (NCMRR) housed within the National Institute of Child Health and Human Development. **From this study, the Commissioners unanimously agreed that the best possible mechanism to address the urgent needs of American society would be a National Center within an existing Institute of the National Institutes of Health.**

Therefore:

The Commission recommends that the Congress authorize the establishment of and appropriate sufficient funds to support a national center for research and education on sleep and sleep disorders to be housed within an existing NIH Institute. The Center's activities will complement the sleep and sleep disorder related research currently undertaken by the various National Institutes of Health, and, through its own award authority, shall encourage and support gap-filling and cross-cutting research, and develop new research programs and educational/training initiatives in the field. In 1992, the Commission recommended that $16.4 million be appropriated for the establishment of this Center.

Update 1995: The National Center on Sleep Disorders Research has been established within the National Heart Lung Blood Institute of the NIH. The Honorable Mark Hatfield, Senior Senator from the state of Oregon, and a committed supporter of sleep disorders research, introduced the enabling legislation in January of 1993. Today, the center has no designated funding although it does have a permanent director. It has made only modest progress in addressing the sleep related problems in our society, but its capacity to mount programs is pitifully weak compared to the size of the problems.

• Training and Career Development

The Commission identified a serious absence of career and training opportunities for young investigators interested in the field of sleep. Research is essential for cures and better treatments of sleep disorders. Currently, the important research questions far outnumber the available trained investigators. Students need to be exposed to sleep medicine in school; additional laboratories and resources are needed to support doctoral and postdoctoral candidates in sleep science.

Therefore:

The Commission recommends that substantially increased levels of federal support be directed to the NIH, the Centers for Disease Control, and other agencies specifically for sleep and sleep disorder research training and career development opportunities.

A number of research training and career development mechanisms are already in place across the NIH. By utilizing these mechanisms, a broadened cadre of researchers can be brought to the field of sleep and sleep disorder research. **To accomplish this goal, the Commission recommends an immediate increase in research training and career development of $2.5 million above existing levels.**

Update 1995: We are unaware of any increase over a very tiny program that was ongoing before the National Commission was created by the Congress.

• Education of Health Professionals

Consistent with its mandate to improve public health, the Public Health Service supports excellent research and promotes the dissemination of research findings to the public through the conduit of the health professionals. At present, the American public is *not* receiving the benefits of new findings on sleep disorders. Ninety-five percent of victims remain undiagnosed, largely because health professionals have not had the opportunity to learn about sleep disorders and sleep deprivation. There is an urgent need for physicians, nurses, and all health care professionals to be able to identify and refer or treat patients with sleep disorders.

Therefore:

The Commission recommends that Congress encourage and support broader awareness of and training in sleep and sleep disorders spanning the full range of health care professions, particularly at the primary care level.

Broader clinical education about sleep and sleep disorders is warranted for physicians, nurses, and others providing clinical health care to Americans of all ages. Because primary care physicians represent the first line of treatment for most citizens, special emphasis should be placed on improving the quality and extent of their training in sleep and sleep disorders. **The Commission recommends the addition of an annual appropriation of $4 million in new dollars to support these activities.**

Update 1995: Today, medical school teaching remains at the same level of stagnant ineffectiveness described by the National Commission after its exhaustive study of medical school curricula in 1991. Consequently, vast numbers of severely ill sleep disorder victims remain unrecognized; and sadly, even if recognized, sleep disorders are often badly mismanaged by unqualified personnel. There are communities in America today where sleep disorders, including obstructive sleep apnea, are highly prevalent and yet entirely unrecognized.

• An Educated America

The nationwide low level of awareness of the nature and impact of sleep disorders and sleep deprivation is a national emergency. Witnesses asked repeatedly, "How many preventable deaths are going to occur this year?" "Why don't we do something right now?" "Why don't we save as many lives as possible now—not years or decades from now?" The Commission has concluded that the American public has been inappropriately denied the benefits of the research knowledge its tax dollars have supported. This situation must be remedied without delay.

Therefore:

The Commission recommends that a major public awareness/education campaign about sleep and sleep disorders be undertaken immediately by the federal government.

Critically important to the Center's mission are the development and implementation of a major public awareness and education campaign about sleep and sleep disorders and the stimulation of greater knowledge of and training in sleep and sleep disorders among health care professionals. Among the primary goals of this campaign are to heighten public awareness and understanding of sleep and sleep disorders, including, but not limited to such issues as the ramifications of sleep deprivation, the nature of sleep disorders, the promotion of healthful behaviors regarding sleep, and the recognition of when a sleep problem will benefit from intervention by a qualified health care professional. The Commission believes that such a public awareness/education campaign can effect behavior change, thereby, ultimately, reducing family dysfunction, lost educational opportunities, accidents, lost income, disability, and lost lives. **To support this important public awareness/ education function, the Commission recommends the addition of an annual appropriation of $3.25 million in new dollars to support this effort.**

Update 1995: America remains a vast reservoir of ignorance about sleep deprivation and sleep disorders. With extremely limited resources allocated from its host Institute, the National Center is slowly creating a plan to do something. In 1995, sleep medicine has still failed to achieve a satisfactory penetration of the educational system.

However, one major victory has been achieved, again, by the action of Senator Mark Hatfield. At his instigation, Congress appropriated one million dollars for a *Driver Fatigue and Inattention Initiative* to analyze the role of sleep deprivation and sleep disorders in highway crashes, to develop and test appropriate educational countermeasures, and to develop a strategy and lay the foundation for a public information campaign using a variety of media and other approaches. These activities are intended to be conducted in close cooperation with the National Center on Sleep Disorders Research.

1995 National Commission Update Summary

Each year, the lives of millions of American men, women, and children are disturbed, disrupted, or destroyed by sleep deprivation, sleep disorders, or sleep disturbances. With an incidence and prevalence of staggering proportions, both sleep disorders and sleep disturbances associated with other medical problems exact a tremendous toll on our Nation's population. A range of sleep disorders and disturbances affect as many as one-third of all American adults. Fifty million adults suffer from a specific chronic sleep disorder, such as obstructive sleep apnea, narcolepsy, or severe clinical insomnia. The costs of a sleepy society include lost lives, lost income, disability, lost educational opportunities, accidents, and family dysfunction; other costs raise the toll much higher. The effect on the quality of life for millions of individuals and families is incalculable. **Today, three years after the National Commission on Sleep Disorders Research submitted its final report to the Congress of the United States, pervasive sleep deprivation and untreated and mistreated sleep disorders remain arguably the biggest health problem in America.**

The work of the National Commission has gauged the nature and magnitude of the problems related to sleep, and has identified several inexpensive, doable solutions which would enable policy makers to make rapid progress in solving them. Because it created the National Commission in the first place, it is difficult to understand why Congress has not acted. Given the gigantic numbers, the extremely low costs of effective societal interventions, and the possibility of a miraculous restoration of health for so many Americans, the current situation should be viewed as unacceptable. Congress must make restoring millions of sleep disorders victims to health and productivity and reducing the carnage on the highways national priorities by funding the National Center on Sleep Disorders Research so it can accomplish its mission. The recommendations of the National Commission on Sleep Disorders Research must be implemented.

Finally, it is clear that sleep professionals, sleep disorders patients, and other concerned citizens must make much greater efforts toward mobilizing grass roots activism to achieve these goals. Constituents all over America must make their elected representatives understand these issues and, as a consequence, develop a commitment to do something.

The Walla Walla Story

In response to the problems identified by the National Commission, my friend and sleep specialist colleague, the late German Nino-Murcia, and I undertook a project to train primary care physicians. We chose a 30-physician multispecialty group in Walla Walla, Washington, a small farming community noted for its famous sweet onions, award-winning red wines, and its native son, Drew Bledsoe, quarterback of the New England Patriots. It also happens to be my hometown. At the time, the nearest sleep medicine facility was over 250 miles away and thus not readily accessible.

At the start of the project, we reviewed more than 600 medical records. Numerous complaints of fatigue were noted in these records, but rarely was a sleep history recorded. Of the charts reviewed, only two patients were referred for sleep evaluations—one with obstructive sleep apnea and one with depression. Because the prevalence of obstructive sleep apnea with *unambiguous* symptoms is two to four percent of the population, at least 12 to 24 patients out of this group should have received a diagnosis of obstructive sleep apnea, not to mention other sleep disorders. This lack of recognition on the part of Walla Walla physicians was not surprising; the National Commission on Sleep Disorders Research had already highlighted the lack of primary care involvement.

After the chart review, German and I conducted a two-day training session for interested primary care physicians in Walla Walla. The instruction included basic information on the physiology and pathologies of sleep, diagnostic procedures, and treatment strategies. A respiratory therapist was trained in polysomnographic data acquisition. Initially, polysomnograms recorded in Walla Walla were mailed to German for interpretation.

The physicians then began diagnosing and treating sleep disorders patients with the support of weekly telephone conferences with us. Initially, all cases were discussed in detail, but as the physicians became more comfortable with polysomnogram interpretation and treatment modalities, only the more problematic cases were discussed. Although most cases involved obstructive sleep apnea, other sleep disorders were diagnosed, including restless legs syndrome, narcolepsy, delayed sleep phase syndrome and psychophysiological insomnia.

The results of this demonstration project have been astounding. Within 13 months, more than 200 patients were studied with polysomnography. Of those studied, 88 percent were diagnosed with obstructive sleep apnea and most were treated with continuous positive airway pressure (CPAP). The physicians were amazed at the number of patients with serious sleep disorders. Nearly all of these patients had been established primary care patients whose sleep disorder was only recognized because of the Walla Walla project. Only eight percent of the polysomnograms performed were normal. The Walla Walla physicians in the project have since acquired the skills and experience to treat patients with virtually all sleep disorders on their own. Three physicians have learned to score and interpret polysomnograms and have established a regional sleep center. Currently, eight patients a week undergo evaluation.

The weekly conference continues. Regular attendees include internists and family physicians, a neurologist, a pulmonologist, a psychiatrist, an ENT surgeon, several respiratory therapists and a cardiologist. This multidisciplinary conference is quite useful in clinical decision-making in difficult cases and serves as an educational forum. One internist has found that 50 percent of his practice is now dedicated to the care of patients with sleep disorders.

Lessons to be learned from the Walla Walla project are many. There is a river of sleep disorders flowing past the eyes of primary care physicians every day. We have clearly shown that these patients can be identified and managed, largely within the constraints of office based medical practice. Whereas patients present to sleep medicine specialists with complaints of sleepiness, our experience suggests that patients may instead present to primary care physicians with complaints of fatigue or lack of energy, rather than sleepiness. Primary care physicians need to be aware that the symptom of fatigue may indicate a primary sleep disorder.

Primary care physicians are in an ideal position to diagnose sleep disorders early. The Walla Walla experience also suggests that primary care physicians are in an ideal position to educate patients about sleep as a component of good health and quality of life. Sleep deprivation creates a sleep debt that must be paid off. Many patients are not aware that sleep is the only way to safely pay off a sleep debt. The consequences of inadequate sleep — especially during dangerous, soporific activities such as driving — are horrific. Additionally, patients need to be educated about sleep-inducing properties of small amounts of alcohol in the sleep-deprived person.

During adolescence, the need for sleep does not decrease and may actually increase, yet most adolescents reduce their nightly amount of sleep. Education is compromised as students sleep in class; lives are endangered as students drive home from football games and parties at night. Family physicians and pediatricians are ideally suited to bring this information to the families and schools in their community. By instructing patients in some rather simple rules of sleep hygiene and the consequences of sleep deprivation, many problems can be simply and inexpensively remedied. This is truly preventive medicine.

Sleep disorders permeate primary care patient populations. Intrinsic sleep disorders are chronic, and transient insomnia is ubiquitous. In addition, sleep disorders interact with other co-morbid illness such as atherosclerotic heart disease, heart failure, asthma, headaches, obesity, depression and hypertension. As the gatekeepers of managed care, primary care physicians can and must include sleep disorders in their domain. The Walla Walla project has clearly demonstrated that this is possible, feasible, and rewarding.

Last Things

I view the reissuing of *The Sleepwatchers* as an interim solution to the need for a good book on sleep and sleep disorders for the general public. Although there are many other things worthy of being mentioned, I will save them for another day. I only wish to add a bulletin that Nathaniel Kleitman is alive and well. There was a wonderful session at the 1995 Associated Professional Sleep Societies meeting in Nashville in which the four individuals most responsible for the discovery of REM sleep and for sleep research in the 1950s presented historical comments. And in addition, the assembled sleep community celebrated the hundredth birthday of Professor Kleitman and sang happy birthday to him as a giant cake was wheeled out. All these individuals can now say they sang at Opryland in Nashville, Tennessee. Professor Kleitman presented a paper, Eugene Aserinsky presented a paper, Michel Jouvet presented a paper, and I was the master of ceremonies. The program chairman of this year's meeting said he wanted to do this for posterity, and I countered with "What has posterity ever done for us?" However, it is unlikely that these four individuals will all be present at the same meeting ever again.

The National Institutes of Health are currently in grave danger from the budget cutting axe which means that all sleep research is in grave danger. Americans must wake up not only to the pervasiveness of sleep deprivation and sleep disorders, but to the fact that the best way to contain health care costs is to find causes and cures for illnesses like Alzheimer's disease, schizophrenia, AIDS, cancer, and, of course, narcolepsy, obstructive sleep apnea, and other sleep disorders. If the NIH is destroyed by an uninformed, economy-minded Congress, the gigantic costs of these illnesses will have to be borne forever.

It is worth mentioning that I dictated the first draft of this final chapter in Hong Kong from 2am to 5am in the deserted lobby of the New World Hotel. I had just arrived to make a presentation at the World Congress of Family Practitioners. However, since my visit was only two days, I elected to remain as much as possible on Stanford time. The few people who straggled through the hotel lobby in the wee hours were clearly puzzled by someone wide-awake, pacing around dictating. One or two night owls or jet-lagged family practitioners from other countries stopped and I spent ten or fifteen minutes teaching them about sleep disorders, thus doing my bit for world wide sleep disorders education. The only hitch to my plan was that I had to give my lectures in Hong Kong at 11pm Stanford time, when I am definitely not at my best, and usually in bed. However, I have spoken to primary care groups so many times during my crusade, that the things I must tell them I know by heart, literally word for word. I am sure I can give the talk even when I am very drowsy, if not actually asleep.